T0215285

Digital Media, Sharing and Everyday Life

Digital Media, Sharing and Everyday Life provides nuanced accounts of the processes of sharing in digital culture and the complexities that arise in them. The book explores definitions of sharing, and the roles that our digital devices and the platforms we use play in these practices.

Drawing on practice theory to outline a theoretical framework of sharing practice, the book emphasizes the need for a coherent and consistent framework for sharing in digital culture and explains what this framework might look like. With insightful descriptions, the book draws out the relationship of sharing to privacy and control, the labored strategies and boundaries of reciprocation and our relationships with the technologies which mediate sharing practices.

The volume is an essential read for researchers, postgraduate and undergraduate students in Media and Communication, New Media, Sociology, Internet Studies, and Cultural Studies.

Jenny Kennedy is Postdoctoral Research Fellow at RMIT, Melbourne. She is a core member of the Digital Ethnography Research Centre (DERC). Jenny's research interests cover media practices in everyday life, social discourses around technology use and material culture, especially in domestic contexts.

Routledge Studies in New Media and Cyberculture

For more information about this series, please visit: www.routledge.com/
Routledge-Studies-in-New-Media-and-Cyberculture/book-series/RSINC

Digital Media, Sharing and Everyday Life

Jenny Kennedy

Routledge
Taylor & Francis Group

LONDON AND NEW YORK

First published 2020 by Routledge

2 Park Square, Milton Park, Abingdon, Oxon OX14 4RN
605 Third Avenue, New York, NY 10017

Routledge is an imprint of the Taylor & Francis Group, an informa business

First issued in paperback 2021

Publisher's Note

The publisher has gone to great lengths to ensure the quality of this reprint
but points out that some imperfections in the original copies may be apparent.

Library of Congress Cataloging-in-Publication Data
A catalog record for this book has been requested

ISBN: 978-1-138-48346-0 (hbk)
ISBN: 978-1-03-217680-2 (pbk)
DOI: 10.4324/9781351054782

Typeset in Sabon
by Apex CoVantage, LLC

Contents

Illustrations

Acknowledgements

This book represents the culmination of my PhD work. I began this work in 2009 as a PhD candidate at Swinburne University of Technology under the intellectual guidance of Esther Milne. I could not have asked for a more generous, nor more supportive mentor during that process, and am continually grateful for her friendship.

I also wish to thank Julian Thomas who saw potential in my abilities and offered a position as Postdoctoral Research Fellowship at RMIT, where I was able to complete this book. Julian and colleagues at RMIT—especially the Technology, Communication and Policy Lab and the Digital Ethnography Research Centre (DERC)—have made me feel perfectly at home and provide ongoing inspiration through their own work.

I feel very fortunate to have so many people to thank for their contributions to this book. Special mention goes to Rowan Wilken for his wonderful encouragement and conversations and to Son Vivienne for providing crucial final stage research support. I'm also grateful to Tama Leaver for helping me take the first steps towards turning my PhD work into this book. Thanks too to Yolande Strengers, James Meese, Emily van der Nagel, Brady Robards, Crystal Abidin, Tim Highfield, Nicholas John, and my many academic friends who have made the whole process that much more enjoyable through their presence and helped prod my work along at various stages over the years.

I would like to acknowledge the research support provided by Alexandra Heller-Nicholas, Hannah Withers and Paula Arcari, and to thank my research participants for their contributions.

Lastly, I would like to thank my family and friends who have been extraordinary in their patience and distraction tactics, especially Evelyn who excels at both.

Parts of this book have been published elsewhere, and are reproduced here with permission.

Introduction

Sharing refers to social activities. Sharing is used to describe the giving away or distribution of something in order to benefit another. A person who shares widely is described as generous. A person who is able to share evenly is described as fair. Sharing is often an early lesson in sociability. Young children are taught to share their crayons, toys and sweets with other children. Both the act and object shared is valued and has social significance. The person who receives gains in knowledge or resources while the person who shares gains via the social capital of attributed generosity or fairness. Sharing therefore has moral implications.

Sharing is a communicative practice, where experiences, artefacts, feelings and emotions are imparted to another. Sharing helps social ties and intimate relationships develop through the process of defining and delimiting boundaries. Communicative sharing develops trust; without it a person may be considered withdrawn, cold or even duplicitous. Sharing reflects a set of values related to interdependence and community. For particular communities, such as support groups like Alcoholics Anonymous, sharing is especially therapeutic. It provides attendees with an opportunity to unburden themselves and simultaneously benefits listeners through the offering of advice and inspiration. Sharing is an affirmative practice that involves bearing witness and testimony.

Sharing is an action that is socially purposed, such as distributing, giving or telling. It is also a social activity of togetherness. Experiences and spaces can be shared, although there are boundaries to the degree in which this occurs. For example, a footpath can be shared by both a cyclist and a jogger who momentarily share the same space as they cross one another but who are not engaged in a shared activity. Conversely, a person and her companion jogging alongside one another share both the same space and the same experience. Still, having both space and experience in common does not necessarily mean that either is shared. For example, public transport users make a point of denying the sharing that is taking place between them and other passengers. This says something of the centrality of social relationships to definitions of sharing, as well as the relationality of sharing.

Sharing can also mean having something in common. Cultural definitions of sharing relate to ways of doing, seeing and being. Within cultures, there are shared ideologies or ways of being that govern individual actions and help shape society. For example, religion is culturally shared. Cultural definitions of sharing extend to 'common sense'; that is, the knowledge and experience people within a given culture are assumed to have in common. Those sharing a culturally specific common sense also expect to share rational decision-making and behavioural tendencies. Sharing cultural sensibilities involves agreed morals and values. Cultural definitions of sharing are concerned more with the types of things that are shared than with the way the sharing occurs. This is because cultural definitions of sharing are learned through social immersion. They are often not attributable to a singular action but, rather, are defined through repeated actions, which serve to fortify a particular way of thinking.

Sharing in economic terms is the distribution or division of an object of value. A share means a part or portion of something. Indeed, rooted in Old English (*scearu*), Dutch (*schare*) and German (*schar*), an etymology of the verb *to share* acknowledges this act of participation, division or apportioning in and of a part or portion. The moment of allocation in sharing is called an exchange. The most commoditised process of exchange, the stock market, allocates shares and determines their market value. The economic market where commodities and securities are bought and sold includes the literal trading of shares. Here the value is given greater priority over the division. The term *sharing* is also used to describe processes of distributing a part or portion of something that does not correlate to its market value, thereby negating the commodity value of the object being exchanged. This does not mean that objects shared have no market value but that objects shared are exchanged outside of market values. Sharing then is also the distribution or division of the object where the allocation is of greater significance than the value.

Platform-based enterprises leverage the collaborative culture of sharing into a sharing economy, mobilising resources and goods through an ethics of sharing and through social relations rather than through market infrastructures. Those involved in sharing economy platforms need not be personally involved with one another so the relations can be widely distributed and loosely affiliated.

Sharing is also a political behaviour. It is an engagement with an existing state of affairs, in which the act of sharing may bring about a new equilibrium or disequilibrium. A share in something means to have a part to play, to be able to exert some influence. Those without a share have neither privilege nor agency. Sharing marks out an individual's status in relation to another when the allocation and direction of benefits of an exchange are not equitable to all involved. Sharing is a matter of power and privilege for it bestows power on those holding the higher share and confers privilege to those able to share without compromising status.

Each of these definitions of *sharing* comes into play in a digital communications context. The scope within definitions of sharing for social, cultural, economic and political application is, in part, what makes the social imaginary of sharing so complex. Intricate and multifaceted meanings are expressed in a single confounding term.

This multiplicity provides context to the fundamental questions I answer in this book: In everyday practices of digital media use, what is sharing and how is sharing mediated?

Sharing is a distinct form of communication championed in digital cultures. Through detailed empirical analysis I uncover what people perceive sharing to be and pay close attention to what they describe as sharing. Situated within digital culture, it is essential to address the relationship that technology and digital culture both have with sharing. Relationships with technologies and digital culture are idiosyncratic and burdened with tensions, which contradict social imaginaries of sharing. I explore how individual perceptions and experiences are situated in relation to these competing imaginaries. Taking a socio-material approach, I consider why defining sharing is so problematic, examining the difficulties and limitations of assuming a common understanding of sharing.

These considerations and concerns are integral to the structure of this book. In the following chapters, I demonstrate key social imaginaries of sharing in digital culture.

Two central themes provide the focus for the process of addressing these questions. The first is the technological context for sharing, meaning the technologies which mediate sharing. The second theme is the labour of sharing, showing the work that people do in the performance of sharing practices.

The main argument in this book is that a new theoretical framework is needed to describe sharing practices in digital culture. This new theoretical framework is described in Chapter 3. Through empirical data, this book articulates three further arguments. The first argument is that sharing is an evolving social norm, the second is that sharing requires immaterial and affective labour and the third argument is that reciprocity is a necessary condition of possibility for sharing.

The empirical data come from a study of sharing within the context of everyday practices of digital media use, which constituted my PhD. In this study I examined mediated practices of sharing through three methods: semi-structured interviews, sharing diaries and participatory social maps.

In semi-structured interviews, participants were asked what the term *sharing* meant to them; where, how and with whom they shared; how they thought others may perceive them through their sharing practices; how roles and relationships mediated their sharing practices; and how interfaces such as Facebook mediated their sharing practices.

Prior to their interviews, I asked participants to complete a diary of their sharing practices. The purpose of the sharing diary was to provide rich details of participant practices related to sharing. Each interview began by asking the participant to talk about the sharing diary they had produced, using the diary as an elicitation tool to contextualise the ensuing discussion. During the interview I asked participants to draw a picture that represented their social network. In this research they are called participatory social maps. Like the diary, in the interview the participatory social map acted as an additional elicitation tool. I interacted with the participants as they drew their maps, asking questions and prompting for details. The questions I asked participants as they were drawing their maps were the following: What is your social network? What do you share in this social network and how do you share in these relationships? and Where do you engage with these networks and where do you share with these networks? Constructing a material representation of these practices was particularly useful for discussing intersubjective boundaries, perceived norms and affordances. These details were then abstracted through the interview process into reflective theorisations of the participant's own sharing practices and digitally mediated intimacies.

The study consisted of 22 participants, recruited through convenience and snowball sampling. The participants ranged in age from 18 to 56. All participants resided in Melbourne, Australia, at the time of interviews, which took place between 2011 and 2013. The research sample was not intended to be representative, although it illustrates nuanced experiences of common sharing practices, with variations in digital literacies and degrees of engagement with digital devices. Some participants were intense users of social media and digital devices, while others were active non-users of particular devices or platforms.

What is apparent through my data is how quickly the digital space changes. At the time of data collection, people were grappling with the idea that sharing was something that required 'work'. A 2012 Intel survey conducted at the same time as my data collection also captured the prevalent concerns of digital media use at the time. The majority of those surveyed engaged in online sharing practices. While the report did not give a definition of sharing, the contexts and descriptions provided indicated sharing to be the volunteering of information or content. Many of the survey respondents reported oversharing to be the most problematic behaviour, with over 85% of respondents believing people should be more considered about what they share online and in what way it may affect how others perceive them. Oversharing was considered to be volunteering too many details, especially banal details, or gripes about one's life, yet the survey also identified the centrality of sharing to relationships. Sharing was considered to enable people to feel connected to one another, and many surveyed used sharing information online to stay up to date with loved ones, as well as those once loved. The Intel survey data presented an interesting conundrum: people were frustrated by other's oversharing yet used this oversharing to find out about people they were no longer be in contact with; furthermore, they also claimed not to overshare themselves. The Intel survey indicated ongoing negotiations of what it means to be 'digital':

> The Intel survey results clearly show that we love being connected. Sharing and getting together online are integral parts of building and maintaining relationships. . . . But we're still finding our way when it comes to determining the most appropriate behaviour [sic] in any given situation online. Should I post a picture of my friend's newborn before she does? Is it acceptable to have 3 different online dating profiles? Does your entire social network want to know what you had for dinner last night? The Intel survey results help us to continue building etiquette guidelines for appropriate online behavior and sharing.
>
> (Post cited in Intel 2012)

Furthermore, while the Intel survey indicated that people were sharing, it didn't explain sharing *means*. What we mean by sharing is one of the questions this book seeks to address.

The Structure of This Book

The book is divided into two sections. The first surveys existing arguments on sharing, drawing on a range of sources from popular discourses and the extensive literature on the subject in anthropology, sociology, social psychology, consumer research and economics to situate an understanding of cultures of sharing. Identifying ruptures and resemblances in the various approaches uncovered, I offer a new approach that attends to practice. I explain what this looks like, drawing upon practice theory approaches and socio-material accounts of 'doing' sharing drawn from empirical data to outline a theoretical framework of sharing practice.

Chapter 1 surveys the discourses and imaginaries of sharing, both persistent and emerging, in a networked culture. The chapter shows how a particular imaginary of sharing has been appropriated by specific cultural intermediaries at the cost of understanding the material and affective significance of sharing in everyday life. Rhetorics of sharing are traced back through networked culture's history to emphasise that sharing's evolvement as a social norm precedes social media platforms.

Chapter 2 analyses existing theoretical approaches to sharing. The literature on sharing is diverse, drawing from fields of anthropology, sociology, social psychology, consumer research and economics. It undertakes an examination of gift-giving in order to understand how sharing practices reinforce social relations, an examination of the tensions between cultural and commodity exchanges to highlight the value of what it is that is shared and a consideration of sharing as control in the form of disclosure and studies the resources and rituals underpinning practices of reciprocity. This chapter synthesises existing literature on distinct aspects of sharing in a networked culture and identifies the need for a new approach.

Chapter 2 is the third and final chapter in Section I. This chapter identifies the productiveness of practice theory approaches for understanding sharing. It outlines the approach of practice theorists to social phenomena and discusses this in relation to others who have also adopted a practice theory approach to understanding what people do in relation to media. Through the concepts of symbolic values, materiality, and competencies, this chapter identifies ways of thinking, understanding and feeling about sharing; modes of performing sharing; and ways in which things are shared and thought about sharing, with specific consideration of digital media.

The second section of the book delves more deeply into the empirical data to describe how sharing is practised.

I draw on this original empirical data to reveal detailed descriptions of the symbolic processes of sharing in digital culture and the complexities that arose in them. In particular, this section explores how sharing interacts with privacy and control, the laboured strategies and boundaries of reciprocation and our relationships with the technologies that mediate sharing practices.

Chapters 4, 5 and 6 take a more detailed look at sharing practices based on original empirical data. Chapter 4 looks at the ways in which boundaries are perceived, defined and enacted in sharing practices. By detailing how users 'do' privacy, for example by optimising access to self through sharing and by identifying examples of boundary work in sharing practice, this chapter argues that sharing is an evolving social norm in the process of being negotiated. It examines motivations for seeking privacy related to self and others, as well as challenges to privacy such as learning norms of socially acceptable sharing, sharing which pushes normative boundaries in pursuit of social connection and context shifts which reposition boundaries of sharing. It demonstrates that subjective navigation of boundaries for sharing is complex and fraught with tension, and that such boundaries are in constant flux.

Chapter 5 addresses the laboured strategies of reciprocation in sharing practices. It argues that reciprocity is a necessary condition for the possibility of sharing. It attends to notions of boundaries, immediacy, causality and reciprocity for sharing and identifies the affective labours of sharing, examining equivalence, causality and listening as particular strategies of reciprocity. This chapter demonstrates the necessity of legibility and attentiveness for reciprocity and raises awareness of the expectations, obligations and limitations that complicate this relationship.

Chapter 6 considers the materialities of mediated sharing practices and the participant's perceptions and navigations of these. This chapter pays particular attention to the technologies that mediate sharing practices. It contributes an understanding of how experiences of sharing are framed by these mediating technologies. By examining expectations of connectivity, it identifies simultaneous intimacies of technology and animosities towards them. It also examines broader contexts and 'publics' that mediate sharing.

Reference

Intel 2012c, 'Intel annual mobile etiquette study examines online sharing behaviours around the world', *Intel Corporation*, viewed 9 March 2019, <http://newsroom.intel.com/community/intel_newsroom/blog/2012/09/05/intel-annual-mobile-etiquette-study-examines-online-sharing-behaviors-around-the-world-global-perception-of-oversharing-revealed>.

Section I

1   Pervasive Narratives of Sharing in Digital Culture

Introduction

On the 31 October 2006, the project manager for the newly developed share functionality on Facebook, Chris Hughes, wrote on the platform's public blog,

> Starting today, there are links to share on Facebook planted all across the Internet, from the articles at Time to the videos at Photobucket. Look for links like this all over the Web, making it easy for you to share.
>
> (2006a)

Hughes, a founding member of Facebook, was known as 'the empath' in Facebook circles for his intuition of users rather than code. He saw Facebook as an opportunity to help people share information most efficiently (McGirt 2009). The timing of his announcement was significant. From that point on, share buttons spread like wildfire in online content and apps. While it was a watershed moment, the proliferation of share rhetoric in social media platforms had actually been building for some years; Hughes's 2006 post was in the midst of the adoption period of this terminology (John 2013).

More significant than the timing of this development was the *framing* of the sharing rhetoric. Hughes's second Facebook blog post was titled 'Sharing is Daring' (Hughes 2006b), a pun on the well-worn maxim 'sharing is caring'. Hughes drew on social sensibilities of goodwill by evoking the imagined narrative of a schoolteacher's lesson when he remarked that 'as a mark of due respect to all the kindergarten teachers of the world, go forth and share' while emphasising the boldness (and then newness) in the provocative action of a dare. This framing established by Hughes continued and came to capture the ethos of Facebook. In 2010, Facebook founder and chief executive officer Mark Zuckerberg emphasised the framing of sharing as affective connectivity, stating in one of his few posts on the blog,

> When we started Facebook, we built it around a few simple ideas. People want to share and stay connected with their friends and the

people around them. When you have control over what you share, you want to share more. When you share more, the world becomes more open and connected.

(2010)

Zuckerberg structured sharing as positive, 'open' communication and 'connected' sociability. It was markedly similar to other social media platform statements of the time, such as Twitter's, which also exaggerated the role the platforms play in bringing people together:

> Whether across the world or across the street, Twitter—and more broadly, technology—allows people to view the world through each other's eyes. As a result, we are able to share information and communicate more easily than any time in our past, bringing the world closer.

(Chowdhury 2011)

Social media platforms heavily utilised this 'open' and 'connected' structuring of meaning. The parlance of sharing was purposively harnessed as a way of initiating familiarisation with the practices digital intermediaries afford—socialising with friends and loved ones, networking with others over shared concerns and navigating stories from around the world.

Social media platforms encouraged sharing by employing the term to draw on social imaginaries of connectivity. As powerful political players, platforms were able to construct an imaginary of digital subjects, where being a good neoliberal subject meant sharing through socialisation, networking and navigating. Good subjects posted, updated, liked, tweeted, retweeted and, most important, *shared*. The dominant rhetoric indicated that it was a social responsibility to be available online.

Mythologies of the Internet

While social media platforms dominated the social imaginary of digital culture at the turn of this century, sharing in earlier internet culture was imagined to be a practice oriented towards developing and maintaining social hierarchies and reputations. Speaking on the social provenance of the internet in the late 1990s, Tim Berners-Lee wrote, 'The dream behind the Web is of a common information space in which we communicate by sharing information' (Berners-Lee and Fischetti 1999).

Early computers were expensive and typically shared by users who developed their programs on punch cards while waiting in turn for access. In the 1950s, a new process allowed users to access a single computer with the impression of simultaneous and uninterrupted interaction. The human–computer interaction occurred by rotating through the interacting sequences of multiple users to continuously maximise the capacity of a mainframe computer (Hauben and Hauben 1996; Abbate 1999). This process, called time-sharing, allowed for the economic and equitable distribution of common resources.

Launched in 1969, ARPANET (Advanced Research Projects Agency Network) was a military funded network of time-sharing computers mostly based in universities (Hafner and Lyon 1996; Rosenzweig 1998). Some describe ARPANET as an early peer-to-peer network which birthed the internet through open systems of collective intelligence with identifiable peers providing access to shared resources, motivated by the imaginations of a select few (Malone, Laubacher and Dellarocas 2009). Alternative histories of the internet emphasise the politics of its military origins and application (Sterling 1993; Moschovitis, Poole and Senft 1999; Clarke 2004) or its manifestation from precursive technologies (see Milne 2010, p. 138). Nevertheless, the rationale for building the network was to share resources (Leiner et al. 2009, p. 25).

While early users respected the principles of ARPANET, the lack of a perceived common purpose meant that many saw it simply as a money-saving exercise by the Advanced Research Projects Agency (ARPA) and an intrusion on local researcher requirements. Lawrence Roberts, program manager and office director at the ARPA, describes this clash of intentions as follows:

> [T]he universities were being funded by us, and we said, "We are going to build a network and you are going to participate in it. And you are going to connect it to your machines. . . . So over time we started forcing them to be involved, because the universities in general did not want to share their computers with anybody. They wanted to buy their own machines and hide in the corner. . . . Although they knew in the back of their mind that it was a good idea and were supportive on a philosophical front, from a practical point of view, they . . . wanted their own machine. It was only a couple years after they had gotten on it [ARPANET] that they started raving about how they could now share research, and jointly publish papers, and do other things that they could never do before. All of which was a great boon to them and the artificial intelligence community for sharing information.
>
> (cited in Norberg 1989)

Amidst the tension of coercion and reluctance, the development of networking technologies was socially constituted. Indeed, as Janet Abbate (1999) attests, the development of the internet was 'a tale of collaboration and conflict among a remarkable variety of players' which demonstrated 'how technologies are socially constructed' (p. 3). Examining early histories of the internet reveal that while the internet may now be conceived of as a cohesive, well-defined technology, initially it was shaped through the intersection of many divergent forces—political, social and cultural (for fuller accounts of internet history including the development of specific technological protocols, see Hauben and Hauben 1996; Abbate 1999; Goggin 2004; Banks 2008).

The serendipitous emergence of email shifted the focus of collaboration from resource sharing to communication. Initially used to convey messages to users of the same computer as early as 1965 (i.e., Massachusetts Institute for Technology's Compatible Time-Sharing System, CTSS), the first networked email was sent in 1972. Email introduced a social dimension to the ARPANET, at odds with the interests of the funding institution: 'once the first couple of dozen nodes were installed, email users turned the system of linked computers into a personal as well as a professional communication tool' (Hafner and Lyon 1996, p. 189). Science fiction author and critic Bruce Sterling elaborates further:

> By the second year of operation [. . .] an odd fact became clear. ARPA-NET's users had warped the computer-sharing network into a dedicated, high-speed, federally subsidised electronic post-office. [. . .] Not only were they using ARPANET for person-to-person communication, but they were very enthusiastic about this particular service—far more enthusiastic than they were about long-distance computation.
>
> (1993, n.p.)

By 1973, email accounted for three-quarters of all ARPANET traffic (Hafner and Lyon 1996, p. 194). While the ARPANET sharing imaginary at the time of development focused on resource efficiency, the practices of users exerted a profound paradigm shift that was not anticipated. Les Earnest, a computer scientist at Stanford University, notes,

> I was surprised at the way the use of email took off, but so were the others who helped initiate that development . . . We thought of [the ARPANET] as a system for resource sharing and expected that remote login and file transfers would be the primary uses.
>
> (cited in Abbate 1999, p. 232, endnotes)

Instead, sharing via email and mailing list was used to develop a sense of community and relational ties between ARPANET users. Databases contained lists of topics such as science fiction, which allowed individuals to not only communicate with large groups but also to develop a community identity among geographically disparate people. Increasingly, the resources of the ARPANET were seen to be the community of users rather than the use of remote devices or access to specific programs.

This social dimension of email also drew on existing perceptions of social hierarchies of power. Stephen Lukasik, who directed ARPA from 1971 to 1975, was himself an early advocator of email, and this influenced the practices of those working under him. Program managers perceived that they could develop closer ties with Lukasik by using email and could gain certain advantages in the workplace, such as budgetary rewards. Consequently at 'ARPA's headquarters, the appeal of the network had nothing to do with computers and everything to do with access to power' (Abbate 1999, p. 108).

Even in the early 1970s, illicit file and software sharing as a regular practice in the ARPANET. Earnest recalls the development of file-sharing practices:

> [A] thing that happened a lot in the 1970s was benign theft of soft-ware. We didn't protect our files and found that both programs and data migrated around the net rather quickly, to the benefit of all. For example, I brought the first spelling checker into existence around 1966 but it wasn't picked up by anyone else, whereas the improved version (around 1971) quickly spread via ARPANET throughout the world.
>
> (pers. comm cited in Abbate 1999, p. 101)

Initial sharing of software took place within the closed communities of those who had access to ARPANET. In the early 1970s, computer researchers did not imagine many other people were using their network. Sharing software was a way of developing relationships within their (limited) community with expectations of mutual participation and reciprocity. The files and software shared were perceived to be part of the commons of the community.

During this pre-internet period, the network was still relatively inaccessible to those outside of the pioneering research communities. Built by technologists and researchers, it was also built *for* technologists and researchers and relied on comprehension of access commands and data ranges (Baym 2010). Although the network structure reflected intentions to promote resource sharing through 'open architecture networking' (Leiner et al. 2009, p. 24), access to such structures were limited.

The first significant areas for popular networked sharing were Bulletin Board Systems (BBSes) and USENET. BBSes provided early public access to networked communities. The first public BBSes were established in 1978 by computer hobbyists Ward Christensen and Randy Suess, who met through the Chicago Area Computer Hobbyists' Exchange (CACHE). Users accessed BBSes over a phone line using a modem, meaning they no longer required access to a mainframe computer to participate. BBSes functioned as repositories of files and software and allowed communities of users to read notices and exchange messages similar to contemporary internet forums.

USENET—established in 1979 as a 'poor man's ARPANET' (Quarterman 1990, p. 243)—used the protocols of mailing lists to post messages to discussion networks known as newsgroups (Hauben and Hauben 1996). USENET provided a means of linking those shut out of the ARPANET community. Unlike BBSes, USENET was decentralised, meaning it did not have a centralised server and did not require a dedicated administrator. Any user could create a newsgroup and users could select which newsgroups they wished to participate in. The functionality of sharing computation had been further adapted for communication:

> Computer users flocked to USENET because it offered new possibilities for social interaction, bringing together "communities of interest" whose members might be geographically dispersed and allowing people to participate anonymously if they chose.
>
> (Abbate 1999, p. 201)

Systems for sharing such as BBSes and USENET were developed by users for users, based on existing networking protocols, and it was expected that they would manifest characteristics in keeping with the attributes of community: shared interests, ongoing participation, common resources, reciprocity and shared language (Whittaker, Isaacs and O'Day 1997, p. 137). Further supporting decentralisation, in 1993 Eugene Roshal created a compressed file format called RAR which made the major distribution of files more efficient.

In the late 1990s specifically oriented file-sharing networks such as Napster (launched 1999) and Gnutella (launched 2000) extended the concept of file-sharing behaviour to file reproduction and distribution. A precursor to and trailblazer for current peer-to-peer file-sharing protocols, the music-sharing site Napster allowed users to identify files through a centralised directory, which filtered download requests. File sharing ceased to be viewed as a 'benign' community activity when the recording industry endeavoured to reframe the practice as an unlawful breach of copyright law (Oberholzer-Gee and Strumpf 2010).

Indeed, multiple conflicting discourses of sharing resonate through digital culture. Jessica Litman (2004) positions sharing as a form of 'anarchic volunteerism' where 'untamed' sharing of digital information, files and communication is more effective than paid subscriptions or hardcopy distribution (p. 4). In 'hive-minded' gift economies, resources are exchanged through unspecified obligations with an expectation of satisfaction through participation.

There is a limit to the utility of this framing of sharing. Here sharing applies only to the distribution of specific objects. Litman says, 'Collecting information on the Internet is "learning". Posting information on the net is "sharing". Try exactly the same thing with recorded music and it is "stealing"' (p. 23). The 'sharing' is troubled by the statement of property upon which intense debates persist. To some, *sharing* is a litigious term synonymous with stealing; to others, it is its imprecise and inappropriate association to tangibility that is the issue.

Sharing, stealing, copying: each term conveys a specific set of principles and values, yet stealing and copying are critical points of departure to sharing. The practices they describe are essentially the redistribution of material or immaterial objects and rights to exclusivity. Sharing and stealing of material objects imply reductive qualities in redistribution. Exclusivity is diminished in distribution and limited by the minimum unit of division. Copying of material objects has implications of scale. Exclusivity is also diminished in distribution, although the nature of the copy means that the exclusivity of the original remains intact. Sharing, stealing and copying each have further implications of scale for immaterial objects. For immaterial objects especially, exclusivity is potentially irrelevant, the original risks becoming obsolete. Sharing, stealing and copying are distinguishable by the terms and ownership of control over the scale and exclusiveness of distribution. Sharing is a relinquishing of control, which may be partial. Stealing is a forceful shift in ownership of control. Copying is a relinquishing of control of distribution where ownership of the original remains intact, although the original may no longer be identifiable or worthy of distinction.

In discussions on peer-to-peer file sharing, Matthew David (2010) argues that through the synonymity of sharing, copying and stealing, the act of sharing has become criminalised. Scarcity is threatened by sharing; thus, modes of open distribution are framed as unlawful and criminal to protect those whose interests are best served by scarcity regardless of whether or not the threat is justified. Networked devices and individuals problematise the notion of scarcity where it refers to digital or informational goods. The distributed systems of file sharing distance the software provider from user interactions and infringed or digitally managed files. Property, rights and ownership discourses challenge the monopoly of media conglomerates and so the acts of providing, uploading or downloading controlled media files or even providing the software or service infrastructure for these acts are framed as criminal acts. The networking of these systems of distribution, themselves increasingly distributed so that a particular entity is not identifiable or connectable to a particular act/file, is partly in response to this criminalisation discourse. The criminalisation of peer-to-peer sharing can be read then as a criminalisation of culture (David 2010, p. 9).

Formed in 2001, Creative Commons also purported to popularise sharing. Creative Commons is an organisation that supports the distribution of creative content in 'the commons—the body of work freely available for legal use, sharing, repurposing, and remixing' (Creative Commons nd). Creative Commons release copyright licenses for free public use which allows content creators to identify their preferred reservation of rights against the benefits of public use. A formalisation of social practice, Creative Commons shows the limits of territorial and philosophical presuppositions and the ephemerality of property rights. John Palfrey and Urs Gasser (2008, p. 138) argue that the 'norms of sharing' are immersed in creative modes of interaction and production, which include illegal down-loading and viewing that threaten the legalities of ownership and copy-right and counterpose creativity with copyright law. There is ambivalence between users as to what constitutes creative use and what amounts to copyright infringement.

Peer-to-peer advocate groups attempted to retaliate against the crimi-nalisation of culture by reclaiming the rhetoric of sharing, through their 'sharing is caring' slogans. In much the same way that social media plat-forms have an interest in framing specific practices as sharing, so, too, do peer-to-peer and file-sharing advocates. By emphasising the ubiquity of these practices and situating them within the continuum of user-generated content, they reframe file-sharing practices as normative rather than ille-gal behaviour, implying that it is the legal system seeking to limit them that is out of date rather than the practices that are out of line.

These latter examples demonstrate that practices of semantic leverag-ing are persistent within digital contexts. Social narratives and imagi-naries of sharing have been discursively framed by multiple and varied political and economic actors. Evident within this narrative of early inter-net culture is the provenance of three distinct motivations for sharing: sharing as an economical means of maximising usage of expensive main-frame computers through timesharing, the distribution of content at an unprecedented and unexpected scale and social intensifications through networked sharing.

As I describe in the discussion of the literature in the next chapter, it was not until the rhetorical 'sharing turn' in the mid-2000s that these narratives were mobilised into particular discourses which each frame technologically situated sharing in a particular way.

References

Abbate, J 1999, *Inventing the internet*, MIT Press, Cambridge, MA.

Banks, MA 2008, *On the way to the web: The secret history of the internet and its founders*, Apress, New York, NY.

Baym, N 2010, *Personal connections in the digital age*, Polity Press, Malden, MA.

Berners-Lee, T and Fischetti, M 1999, *Weaving the web: The original design and ultimate destiny of the world wide web by its inventor*, Harper, San Fran-cisco, CA.

Chowdhury, A 2011, 'Global pulse', *Twitter weblog*, viewed 6 March 2019, <http://blog.twitter.com/2011/06/global-pulse.html>.

Clarke, R 2004, 'Origins and nature of the internet in Australia', in G Goggin (ed), *Virtual nation: The internet in Australia*, UNSW Press, Sydney.

Creative Commons nd, 'Use & remix', *Creative commons*, viewed 6 March 2019, <https://creativecommons.org/use-remix/>.

David, M 2010, *Peer to peer and the music industry: The criminalization of shar-ing*, Sage, London.

Goggin G (ed) 2004, *Virtual nation: The internet in Australia*, UNSW Press, Sydney.

Hafner, K and Lyon, M 1996, 'Casting the net', *The Sciences*, vol. 36, no. 5, pp. 32–36.

Hauben, M and Hauben, R 1996, *Netisens: On the history and impact of usenet and the internet*, IEEE Computer Society Press, Los Alamitos, CA.

Hughes, C 2006a, 'Share is everywhere', *The Facebook blog*, viewed 31 October 2012, <http://blog.facebook.com/blog.php?post=2215537130>.

Hughes, C 2006b, 'Sharing is daring', *The Facebook blog*, viewed 27 October 2012, <http://blog.facebook.com/blog.php?post=2214737130>.

John, NA 2013, 'Sharing and web 2.0: The emergence of a keyword', *New Media & Society*, vol. 15, no. 2, pp. 167–182.

Leiner, BM, Cerf, VG, Clark, DD, Kahn, RE, Kleinrock, L, Lynch, DC, Postel, J, Roberts, L G and Wolff S 2009, *Brief history of the internet*, viewed 6 March 2019, <www.internetsociety.org/internet/what-internet/history-internet/brief-history-internet>.

Litman, J 2004, 'Sharing and stealing', *Hastings Communications and Entertainment Law Journal*, vol. 27, no. 1, pp. 1–48.

Malone, T, Laubacher, R and Dellarocas, C 2009, 'Harnessing crowds: Mapping the genome of collective intelligence', *MIT Sloan Research Paper No. 4732-09*.

McGirt, E 2009, 'How Chris Hughes helped launch Facebook and the Barack Obama campaign', *Fast company*, 1 April, viewed 6 March 2019, <www.fastcompany.com/1207594/how-chris-hughes-helped-launch-facebook-and-barack-obama-campaign>.

Milne, E 2010, *Letters, postcards, email: Technologies of presence*, Routledge, London.

Moschovitis, CJ, Poole, H and Senft, TM 1999, *History of the internet: A chronology, 1843 to the present*, ABC-CLIO, Santa Barbara, CA.

Norberg A 1989, 'An interview with Lawrence Roberts', *Charles Babbage Institute*, Minnesota, http://conservancy.umn.edu/bitstream/107608/1/oh159lgr.pdf.

Oberholzer-Gee, F and Strumpf, K 2010, 'File sharing and copyright', in J Lerner and S Stern (eds), *Innovation policy and the economy*, vol. 10, University of Chicago Press, Chicago, IL, p. 1955.

Palfrey, J and Gasser, U 2008, *Born digital: Understanding the first generation of digital natives*, Basic Books, Phoenix, AZ.

Quarterman, JS 1990, *The matrix: Computer networks and conferencing systems worldwide*, Digital, Bedford, MA.

Rosenzweig, R 1998, 'Wizards, bureaucrats, warriors and hackers: Writing the history of the internet', *American Historical Review*, vol. 103, pp. 1530–1552.

Sterling, B 1993, 'Short history of the internet', *The Magazine of Fantasy and Science Fiction*, vol. 84, no. 2, pp. 99–107.

Whittaker, S, Isaacs, E and O'Day, V 1997, 'Widening the net', *SIGCHI Bulletin*, vol. 29, no. 3, pp. 27–30.

Zuckerberg, M 2010, 'Making control simple', *The Facebook blog*, viewed 27 May 2013, <http://blog.facebook.com/blog.php?post=391922327130>.

2 Theories of Sharing

Introduction

Since Malinowski's (1922) description of the Kula ring, conviction in the intrinsic power of exchange has shaped popular and critical imaginaries of sharing. Successive theorists have established the structuring power of sharing in social practices. Exchange and gift theorists, in particular, have attempted to explain how sharing rituals demonstrate social hierarchies and ideologies. Importantly, sharing is shown to be an essential communicative set of practices with social consequences. While a full genealogical account of gift-giving and reciprocity literature is beyond the scope of this book, it is important to note the provenance of key social theories which permeate discussions of sharing.

Conceptual Boundaries: Gift-Giving and Reciprocity

Gift-giving, or gifting, is the socialised practice of exchange which is considered separate or distinct to economic models of exchange. Gift-giving practices are invested with physical, social, psychological and emotional value according to the everyday contexts in which they are situated. In his classic study *The Gift* (1954), anthropologist Marcel Mauss developed his idea of gift-giving from Bronislaw Malinowski's observations on Trobriand culture in *Argonauts of the Western Pacific* (1922). Malinowski studied the system of exchange known as the 'Kula Ring' in the Trobriand Islands. Kula valuables, shell necklaces (*veigun*) and shell armbands (*mwali*), are exchanged in opposite circular directions around the islands in systems demonstrating political authority and status:

> Apart from any consideration as to whether the gifts are necessary or even useful, giving for the sake of giving is one of the most important features of Trobriand sociology, I submit that it is a universal feature of all primitive societies.
>
> (1922, p. 175)

The ritual of giving Kula valuables reveals the social status of both the giver and the recipient. Gift-giving practices are imbued with symbolic capital and power through the obligation to reciprocate. Based on this, Mauss positioned gift-giving within a trifold chain of social obligation: to give, to receive and to give back. The recipient of a gift, Mauss argued, was *obliged* to accept and make a return gesture, enforcing social ties between groups (Parry 1986, p. 457).

Alvin Gouldner (1960) identified three different codes of obligation for reciprocity: interdependent transactions, folk beliefs and moral norms. Interdependent transactions require the mutual actions of one party in response to another. In studies of reciprocal exchanges such as these, it is difficult to determine when the exchange begins, as it often produces a self-perpetuating circle of exchange. Similar to the cultural imaginary, folk beliefs in reciprocity can be found in cultural ideas of people getting what they deserve, karmic retribution and 'just desserts' (Malinowski 1922; Gouldner 1960; Lerner, Skinner and Sorell 1980; Bies and Tripp 1996). Reciprocity is also considered a moral norm (Gouldner 1960), based on the logic of how one *ought* to behave (Moore 2004). Individuals are culturally oriented to respond reciprocally. The degree to which they respond differs across cultures and individuals in their concern for social obligation (Murstein, Cerreto and MacDonald 1977; Clark and Mills 1979; Rousseau and Schalk 2000; Shore and Coyle-Shapiro 2003).

Karl Polanyi (1944) viewed reciprocity as a symmetrical economic form, while Marshall Sahlins (1972) proposed a typology of reciprocity scaled by propinquity (close kinship). For Sahlins, generalised reciprocity is a form of exchange between close agents, such as kinship groups. Conversely, balanced reciprocity (a more economic gift exchange) and negative reciprocity (where the aim is to receive without giving) extend the boundaries of kinship groups (Sahlins 1972).

The generalisation of gift-giving to a trifold process of giving, receiving and reciprocating belies the complex network of processes in which events of gift-giving are embedded (Sherry 1983). George Homans (1958) and John Thibaut and Harold Kelley (1959) proposed that exchange is key to, and ever present in, social interactions:

> Social behavior is an exchange of goods, material goods but also non-material ones, such as the symbols of approval or prestige. Persons that give much to others try to get much from them, and persons that get much from others are under pressure to give much to them. This process of influence tends to work out at equilibrium to a balance in the exchanges.
>
> (Homans 1958, p. 606)

There was (and still is) intense debate over what constitutes gift-giving and how it involves the transferral of ownership of an object from one party to another. Gift-giving was often placed in opposition to commodity exchange, which is the transferral of ownership of one object for another object deemed to be of the same or similar value. Certain scholars have differentiated gift-giving from false gift-giving (or commodity exchange) by looking at the *motivations* of the giver. For example, Lewis Hyde (1983) distinguished between true gift-giving, which he argued is motivated by gratitude, and false gift-giving, which is motivated by obligation. True gift-giving does not require or anticipate reciprocation, whereas false gift-giving does. Like Hyde's true gift, Jacques Derrida's (1987) concept of gift-giving was also not contingent on reciprocity. A gift must be freely given with no expectation of return and without premeditation:

> The gift must be given by chance. If the gift is calculated, if you know what you are going to give to whom, if you know what you want to give, for what reason, to whom, in view of what, etc., there is no longer any gift.
>
> (Derrida 1987, p. 198)

Derrida argued that gift-giving cannot be calculated, expected or expected to be returned.

Economic anthropologist Stephen Gudeman proposed that one of the essential elements missing from discussions of reciprocity is community:

> Sharing is the act of making and maintaining community, and without it there can be no reciprocity. Allotment does not come 'after' reciprocity; rather, moments of reciprocity or the gift are tokens of existent community and a mode of allotment.
>
> (2001, p. 86).

Applying his argument to contemporary and historical studies of markets and primitive societies, Gudeman posited that both communal and commercial values are allotted within communities. Reciprocity and the relationships engendered through reciprocity are neither separate nor opposed to economy (Gudeman 2001, p. 81).

For Gudeman, reciprocity and gifts function to extend the limits of community to those not currently within the dyadic limits, meaning that the gift extends the boundaries of community to those outside, to whom the gift is offered: 'the gift is a foray across group boundaries. It connects social worlds or islets of incommensurability within a plural universe' (Gudeman 2001, p. 92). Reciprocation of the gift is a token of participation and/or inclusion into that boundary of community, and it also extends the boundaries of the reciprocating community. The 'spirit' of the gift is the extension of commons (both goods and people) outside of a group, thus extending the base of a community (Mauss 1954, p. 14).

Reciprocity in these terms is a social process of balancing social values. Such processes are not without tensions, including those between individual basic needs and community, distance and proximity and privacy and publicness. As I demonstrate in the chapters in Section II, these tensions continue to resonate through practices of sharing in digital culture.

Historically, tensions have also existed among theorists surrounding the materiality of a gift. For instance, there is some ambiguity in the academic literature about what constitutes a gift. Erving Goffman (1971) suggested a gift is a relationship signal, while David Cheal (1987) argued that affective objects such as love and trust are gifts of expression. The value or definition of a gift is both contextual and dynamic. John Sherry (1983) argued, 'The transformation from resource to gift occurs through the vehicles of social relationships and giving occasions' (p. 160). Similarly, Hyde (1983) stated that a 'gift that cannot move loses its gift properties' (p. 9). Jacques Godbout and Alain Caillé (1992) contended that if an object does not reinforce or create social ties, then it is not a gift. Others argued that gifts are normative ideas, judgements and expressions of taste (Berking 1999). Arjo Klamer defined a gift as follows:

A generous interpretation of the gift considers a gift any 'good', including money, that is transferred, conveyed or transmitted from one party to another when the nature, the value and the timing of the return of an equivalent is left undetermined.

(2003, p. 243)

While exchange and gift theorists have struggled to articulate a singular definition of a gift, they have nonetheless been able to distinguish between the types of objects that may be gifted or exchanged. Social exchange theorists Edna Foa and Uriel Foa (2012) identified six resources, or objects, which can be exchanged: love, status, information, money, goods and services. These objects were understood according to how particular they are (where value is relative to source) and the concreteness of the object (whether it is tangible or symbolic). The particularity or concreteness of an object also affects how it is exchanged, as well as the context of the exchange (Foa and Foa 2012; also Martin and Harder 1994; Chen 1995). Foa and Foa's typology is still productive for examining the materiality of sharing practices, and I return to their typology in the next chapter.

Foa and Foa's typology allowed for different types of objects being exchanged in different sorts of relationships. It was also acknowledged that the same objects could be exchanged in different ways in the same sorts of relationships. Linda Molm described the purpose of exchange as providing 'tangible goods and services but also capacities to provide socially valued outcomes such as approval or status' (2003, p. 2). She continued: 'Actors seek to obtain more of the outcomes that they value and others control, and they do so through the processes of social exchange'

(2003, p. 2). As with rules, different relationships and roles were seen to play a part in the types of objects that are exchanged (Blau 1964). Chao Chen (1995) and Joanne Martin and Joseph Harder (1994) indicated that objects are exchanged in different ways under different circumstances. So while social exchange theory may have said something about the types of exchanges that occur, and the types of objects that may be exchanged, it has said little about the contexts of exchange, such as specificities of how particular relationships may involve particular objects being shared in a particular manner of exchange or how practices are situated by sociocultural contexts.

The digitisation of cultural objects added another layer of complexity to networks of exchange that the preceding literature could not fully address.

The Sharing Turn

Across accounts of digital culture, there are conflating definitions of sharing. Here, cultural objects can be shared without reduction and the mass sharing of content—be it through peer-to-peer, social media platforms, wikis and so on—brings a wider number of actors into the network of labour exchange. However, while digital objects may be 'limitless', the resources to make the sharing social (i.e., immaterial or affective labour) are finite. Second, the resources to convey gifts (bandwidth, server space, etc.) are also limited. Hence, social media platforms afford opportunities to limit or make content scarce, both socially and technically (Skågeby 2008, pp. 296–297). In order to add precision and nuance to the field, I untangle definitions of digital culture practices by identifying three distinct narratives: sharing as an economy, sharing as a mode of scaled distribution and sharing as a site of social intensification. Most significantly, this demonstrates the contradistinctions among these discourses, which are often considered a single body of literature. Rather than collapsing the variegated and rich meanings and practices, I map the discursive threads to provide a framework for a theory of sharing.

Sharing as an Economy

Sharing as an economy is a significant thread in the literature on collaborative consumption and participatory culture. Sharing in this context refers to access to services or resources without ownership (this is not to say that monetary exchanges are absent). Broadly, this discourse engages with the way in which commodities are valued and distributed in a networked culture and often frames such exchanges in relation to gift-giving.

In digital culture, there is both connection and tension between gift-giving and commodity exchange principles. Commodities hold 'a particular type of social potential' (Appadurai 1986, p. 6). The gift economy is one which places emphasis on social motives to move objects rather than economic motives (Jenkins, Ford and Green 2013). Social and economic motives are often counterpoised in a networked culture, although gift-giving and commodity exchanges, in fact, occur alongside each other (Benkler 2004, 2006; Leadbeater 2008; Shirky 2010). For example, Nancy Baym (2011 p. 22) identifies in her analysis of gift-giving practices in music communities that networked culture amplifies tensions between gift-giving and commodity exchange. As Hyde (1983) rightly argues in relation to art practices in market societies, there is a need for gift-giving to be reconciled with commodity exchange, to show how these are interdependent and concurrent practices yet enabled by distinct motivations.

Henry Jenkins, Sam Ford and Joshua Green (2013) state that 'gift economies are relatively dynamic in terms of the fluid circulation of goods, while commodity cultures are relatively dynamic in terms of the fluid social relations between participants' (p. 52). In commodity exchanges, the value of the goods is somewhat stabilised; it is the relationships of those engaged in the exchange process that are in flux. Conversely, in gift economies, relationships are 'stabilised' through ongoing gift-circulation practices, which continuously transform the value of the objects being circulated. These distinctions are problematic in regards to the sharing economy, which similarly destabilises the value of goods, although does not necessarily stabilise relationships as a consequence.

The sharing economy is a socio-technical system for the exchange of goods and services. It refers to a collection of services that enable private and commercial owners of particular resources to make them available to others. Internet-based services aggregate assets and services for access. The broadest definitions of the sharing economy include object-oriented systems which 'rent' access to particular objects or facilities—that is, washing machines (www.streetbank.com), spare bedrooms (www.airbnb.com), cars (www.flexicar.com.au); redistribution systems that shift ownership of an object from one person to another, that is, www.freecycle.com; and collaborative lifestyle systems where amenities such as workspaces or skills are shared, that is, www.deskcamping.com or www.byfork.com. The sharing economy therefore emphasises collaborative consumption, non-ownership models of temporary access to resources and the reliance on internet technologies to coordinate access.

Digital technologies are hailed as providing a means of effectively and efficiently connecting those requiring access to a particular shareable good to those with the resources required at such a scale that the model becomes economically viable as an alternative to commodity exchange (Botsman and Rogers 2010). Importantly, sharing economy literature uses the language of sharing rather than gift-giving to describe practices of consumption to imply community-fostering practices and altruistic 'neighbourly' values, emphasising the notion that relationships are stabilised through participation. Terms used over the decade to describe the same phenomena include 'commercial sharing systems' (Lamberton and Rose 2012), 'co-production' (Humphreys and Grayson 2008), 'co-creation' (Lanier and Schau 2007), 'consumer participation' (Fitzsimmons 1985) and 'online volunteering' (Postigo 2003). Each of these terms is specifically employed in relation to imaginaries of sharing; however, it is questionable whether such systems actually stabilise or intensify social relations.

One reason such systems may not stabilise social relations is the non-necessity of reciprocation. There is a distinction between compensation and reciprocity; the sharing economy holds an expectation of compensation. The difference between compensation and reciprocity is based on ownership and control. Compensation requires a counter-transferal of ownership, whereas reciprocity confirms an extension of control: having agency over future practices of exchange or processes of circulation.

Belk (2007, 2010, 2013) suggests that commodity exchange, gift-giving and sharing form part of a continuum, with commodity exchange and sharing at the extremes. Belk sees sharing as not requiring reciprocation, while gift-giving and commodity exchange do. Thus, Belk (2007, p. 128) positions sharing as a practice that makes no attempt at material balance or compensation. For Belk, sharing is a practice that involves 'the act and process of distributing what is ours to others for their use *and/or* the act and process of receiving or taking something from others for our use' (2007, p. 126, emphasis mine). Indicated in the 'and/or' of Belk's description of sharing (he avoids calling it a definition of *sharing*, which further points to the complexities and difficulties inherent in the term), is the non-necessity of reciprocity or compensation. According to Belk, there is also a significant difference between the three in relation to the transferral of ownership, which he argues occurs in gift-giving and commodity exchange but not in sharing.

Framing activities within a networked culture as consumption behaviours, Belk (2010) critiques how sharing has been theorised in distinction to gift-giving and commodity exchange. Belk attributes the reluctance to study sharing to the subsumption of sharing into conceptual models of gift giving or commodity exchange—indeed, much of the literature he cites uses the language of each interchangeably—together with the interiority and ubiquity of sharing practices (p. 716). These reasons also present challenges for defining sharing. Belk distinguishes between conceptual boundaries through prototypes rather than 'taxonomic definitions' in order to counter the imprecision of existing definitions of sharing.

Ultimately, then, across this literature overview it is clear that much of what is described as the sharing economy is not actually sharing. Transferals of ownership or compensation do not occur in practices of sharing. The sharing economy occupies a space between sharing and commodity exchange markets in which transferal of ownership and compensation occurs.

Sharing as Scaled Distribution

A second way sharing in a networked culture is problematically framed is in terms of scale. Digital technologies provide opportunities to scale the sharing of digital ephemera to a massive volume. In relation to peer-to-peer sharing and user-generated content, sharing is burdened by the properties of digital cultural objects that are multiplied rather than divided, which blur the line between producer and consumer, and whose related processes of copying, distributing, accessing and altering run counter to economic models of scarcity (Stalder and Sützl 2011, p. 2).

Sharing in this context involves an *extension* of ownership rather than a transferal. The term *file sharing* can be located in the history of networked culture (John 2017); however, it derives from the digital nature of the process rather than social practices. From time-sharing to shared file and disk access, file sharing has always been a principle of networked culture. Nevertheless, this has been met with opposition from some quarters, prompting the ongoing 'war on sharing' (Stallman 2009), where various legislative bodies and stakeholders debate rights of distribution, signalled by contesting terminology, that is, *piracy* and *file sharing*. Similarly, the term *piracy* incites imagery of a violent transferal of ownership, perpetuated by the notion that works of art 'bleed' if they are shared (Aigrain 2012, p. 22). Economist Stan Liebowitz (2006) says, 'File sharing is a misnomer because file-sharers do not experience these files together nor are they likely to ever meet or even know one another' (p. 4). This comment makes reference to an assumption of the centrality of social relations in sharing practices and emphasises the distributive processes of file sharing over the social.

There are therefore two critical tensions in the discourse of sharing as scaled distribution, which emerge in such debates on file sharing. The first is its supposed disconnect from the social. Reputation is, in fact, shown to be significant to users of file sharing technologies, who are often pseudonymous rather than anonymous (Marti and Garcia-Molina 2003). The second is the conflict with commodity markets. File sharing is often framed as another form of gift-giving (e.g., Cenite et al. 2009) because it occurs separately from market principles of commodity exchange, which as we have seen are conceptualised as mutually exclusive. Cynics claim that file sharing detracts from and directly threatens the commodity market by removing thresholds of scarcity, though this is shown not to be the case (e.g. the Swedish Model; see Baym 2011).

Relatedly, there is interest in the devices and platforms that afford sharing practices. The digital properties of technology operate as both intermediaries and mediators (Latour 2007). As intermediaries, technologies (and their users) transport and distribute content and meaning without altering their original properties, that is file sharing. Distribution and multiplication of digital content require little monetary or labour cost. The cost instead resides in the production, which occurs at a different site. Additionally, while distribution has the potential to enact social relations, it is not essential or guaranteed. As mediators, technologies provide opportunities to transform, distort or modify digital content in the process of distribution. For example, mailing lists, blogs, discussion boards and fandom mash-up forums are sites of both production and distribution (Jenkins 1992; Leadbeater and Miller 2004; Shirky 2008). The labour of production is downplayed as 'creativity', through which users become producers or 'produsers' rather than consumers (Bruns 2008). As producers, social relations are central to users of mediator technologies.

There is also a distinction between the types of immaterial objects that are scaled up in distribution. Social media platforms, peer-to-peer file sharing, peer production and mass collaboration afford large-scale intellectual and affective sharing. Large-scale intellectual sharing is framed as innovative (Rheingold 2002; Weber 2004; Tapscott and Williams 2008), typified by Wikipedia, open-source software and open publishing. When intellectual immaterial objects are shared *en masse*, the contribution to the digital commons is often celebrated (von Hippel 2005; Benkler 2006; Reagle 2010). However, when affective immaterial objects are scaled up in distribution, the reaction is highly cautionary and interspersed with tales of social solitude and meaningless engagement (Turkle 2011). Large-scale affective sharing raises broader questions about community.

Sharing as Social Intensity

The third significant discursive thread of sharing in digital culture is that of social intensification. Belk (2010) proposes mothering and family allocations of resources as the prototypes of sharing. Sharing is motivated by an extension of self and familial relationships.

For Belk, there are two directions for sharing: 'sharing in' and 'sharing out' (2010). Sharing is a cultural process of community inclusion (for example, having a drink with friends), whereas sharing out creates no social ties (for example, car-share initiatives). Both of these examples of sharing are also practices of resource consumption.

Sharing is defined in relation to disclosure and affect, meaning to make oneself available to others through some form of sentiment articulation. This framing is central to debates on social connectivity and immaterial and affective labour, especially where enabled through social media platforms, which vigorously advocate the discourse (John 2017; Kennedy 2013). As Andreas Wittel (2011) accurately claims, the social discourse of sharing is distinct to the other narratives of sharing already described. Sharing has the potential to intensify the social: 'the decision to share will generally produce an intensification of social activity and social exchange' (Wittel 2011, p. 5). The sharing of material objects requires some form of social activity, while the sharing of immaterial objects, whether intellectual or affective, is considered to be inherently social:

> Whereas the sharing of material things produces the social (as a consequence), the sharing of immaterial things is social in the first place. Whether we share intellectual things such as thoughts, knowledge, information, ideas, and concepts, or affective things such as feelings, memories, experiences, taste, and emotions, the practice of sharing is a social interaction.
>
> (Wittel 2011, p. 5)

If the sharing economy's purpose is to redistribute access to resources and services without redistributing ownership, and the purpose of sharing as scaled distribution is to extend ownership, then affective sharing's purpose is to provoke social intensification (and the political economy that thrives through such practices). Social intensification or sociability has always been a key purpose in online communities (Rheingold 1993; Preece 2000), where intellectual and affective objects are shared as well as material culture (Baker 2012). Communities are constructed around the identities, relationships and communicative practices of members (Baym 1995; Katz et al. 2004), where exchanges among members intensify social bonds.

Nevertheless, frameworks of sharing are still fraught with tensions, particularly in relation to terms of privacy and disclosure. These tensions are pervasive in debates on networked culture in which users of social media platforms share personal details about themselves as a condition of access to such platforms. Early studies of disclosures in social media platforms show the challenges users face in sharing (e.g., Donath and boyd 2004; Barnes 2001). The multiplicity of social contexts—referred to as 'context collapse' (Wesch 2009)—requires that people employ a range of strategies such as sharing different content, withdrawal or censorship of content. Despite perceived risks, and despite the shifting nature of privacy policies on platforms such as Facebook, people do share through social media platforms. Prior research has also illustrated the social motivations of these practices. For example, Nancy Collins and Lynn Miller (1994) found a direct correlation between those who disclose and those who are 'liked'. These examples reinforce that these tensions in sharing practices precede social media platforms.

When attempting to define sharing, it is important to consider each of these three distinct narratives of sharing in unison. Yet given there are overlaps between them, the precise boundaries of each are conceptually fluid: both sharing as an economy and sharing as a mode of scaled distribution may also affect social intensification, and sharing as social intensification may have implications for the scale of content and the access to resources or services. A further problem with sharing, as it is discussed in each of these contexts, is that it is discursively wrapped up with other terms such as gift-giving, exchange and disclosure. Having demonstrated how conceptual boundaries of sharing are problematically fluid, I now turn to those who have made an effort to define these boundaries.

Interrogations of Sharing in Digital Culture

Sharing as a communicative model in digital culture has received growing critical interrogation over the last decade (Stalder and Sützl 2011; Wittel 2011; John 2017; van Dijck 2013; Meikle 2014).

Further indicating that the disciplinary focus of his work is on the consumption of resources, Belk overlooks the political economy of sharing in a networked culture. For example, he describes the internet as a 'consumption phenomenon' (2010, p. 720) and states, 'By transcending the perspective that information is something to be owned, brought, and sold, Flickr, YouTube, Facebook, Google, and many other such sites have ushered in a new era of sharing that has quickly been embraced by millions' (p. 715). Belk omits that in 'transcending' the commodity exchange of information, the exchange of information data and immaterial labour of sharing on such sites is itself transformed into a commodity to be exchanged. Interestingly, Belk characterises this sharing as nonreciprocal. In opposition to this, Bart Cammaerts' (2011) analysis of sharing in a networked culture concludes that 'all forms of digital sharing involve degrees of reciprocity', although at times he conflates sharing with gift-giving. Cammaerts further argues that commodity exchange has been disrupted by gift-giving and sharing, with specific examples given of sharing code, content and access. However, these practices of sharing, discussed in more detail in the section that follows, become 'enmeshed with capitalist logics' and, in fact, become 'sources of commercial exploitation' (p. 58).

In her 2013 book *The Culture of Connectivity*, Jose van Dijck devotes a chapter on Facebook to the negotiation of sharing norms. Van Dijck (2013) states, 'sharing is often pitched against the legal term "privacy"' (2013, p. 46), yet, she argues, it is the norms of sharing that are being negotiated, by platforms and users alike, with privacy a condition of that negotiation. These norms reflect sharing as both the purposeful distribution of personal information, codified in the interface and algorithms, as well as the channelling of aggregated data to commercial (and government) parties. Van Dijck identifies sharing as an essentially ambiguous term: 'Whereas the term "privacy" commonly refers to the judicial realm, "sharing" involves social as well as economic norms, cultural as well as legal values' (p. 46). Similarly problematising the evolving norms of sharing—albeit more sensationally—Ben Agger's book *Oversharing* (2012) paints a lurid image of the dangers of negotiating new norms and the consequences for privacy. For instance, Agger raises concerns over 'how oversharing reflects and reproduces certain personality disorders that hinder people's attempts to be happy' and that 'oversharing in 160-character texts and even shorter tweets causes public discourse to decline', seeking instead 'ways to transform our pornographic public sphere, in which people bare their bodies and their innermost thoughts and desires' (p. xii).

Nicholas John (2017) traces the term *sharing* as a keyword in the Raymond Williams sense and as a dominant framework of social engagement in digital culture. John argues that sharing permeates all activity in digital contexts. He tracks the conceptual slippage of sharing across three spheres: intimate relationships, social media and sharing economies. He argues that the reason the concept of sharing plays a heavy role in constituting digital culture is through this slippage, which naturalises ideological narratives of sharing.

What is most compelling about these prior interventions is the centrality of social relations to sharing, the positioning of sharing as a cultural value that highlights the ongoing negotiations of normative aspects of sharing as a cultural practice and the evidential—if not foregrounded—interplay of sociotechnical features. Observed throughout these discussions is the difficulty of pinning down the meaning of sharing. As discussed so far, the literature provides a spectrum of descriptions of some characterisations or features of sharing, yet the question of what sharing is remains both profound and elusive.

Through this synthesis of the literature on technologically situated sharing, I extend understanding of how sharing is discursively framed, in relation to other forms of exchange, and showed how the 'turn' towards sharing has, in fact, taken three distinct paths, none of which address critical gaps in the conceptual framework of sharing practices.

References

Agger, B 2012, *Oversharing: Presentations of self in the internet age*, Routledge, New York, NY.

Aigrain, P 2012, *Sharing: Culture and the economy in the internet age*, Amsterdam University Press, Amsterdam.

Barnes, B 2001, 'Practice as collective action', in TR Schatzki, K Knorr-Cetina and E von Savigny (eds), *The practice turn in contemporary theory*, Routledge, London and New York, NY, pp. 17–28.

Baym, N 1995, 'The emergence of community in computer-mediated communication', in M Smith and P Kollock (eds), *Communities in cyberspace*, Routledge, London, pp. 138–163.

Baym, N 2011, 'The Swedish model: Balancing markets and gifts in the music industry', *Popular Communication*, vol. 9, no. 1, pp. 22–38.

Belk, R 2007, 'Why not share rather than own?', *Annals of the American Academy of Political and Social Science*, vol. 611, no. 1, pp. 126–140.

Belk, R 2010, 'Sharing', *Journal of Consumer Research*, vol. 36, no. 5, pp. 715–734.

Belk, R 2013, 'You are what you can access: Sharing and collaborative consumption online', *Journal of Business Research*, vol. 67, no. 8, pp. 1595–1600.

Benkler, Y 2004, 'Sharing nicely', *Yale Law Journal*, vol. 114, no. 2, pp. 273–358.

Benkler, Y 2006, *The wealth of networks: How social production transforms markets and freedoms*, Yale University Press, New Haven, CT.

Berking, H 1999, *Sociology of giving*, Sage, London.

Bies, RJ and Tripp, TM 1996, 'Beyond distrust: "Getting even" and the need for revenge', in RM Kramer and TR Tyler (eds), *Trust in organizations: Frontiers of theory and research*, Sage Publications, Inc., Thousand Oaks, CA, pp. 246–260.

Blau, PM 1964, *Exchange and power in social life*, Wiley, New York.

Bruns, A 2008, *Blogs, Wikipedia, second life, and beyond: From production to produsage*, Peter Lang Publishers, New York.

Cammaerts, B 2011, 'Disruptive sharing in a digital age: Rejecting neoliberalism?', *Continuum: Journal of Media & Cultural Studies*, vol. 25, no. 1, pp. 47–62.

Cheal, D 1987, 'Showing them you love them: Gift giving and the dialectic of intimacy', *Sociological Review*, vol. 35, no. 1, pp. 150–169.

Chen, CC 1995, 'New trends in rewards allocation preferences: A Sino-U.S. comparison', *Academy of Management Journal*, vol. 38, pp. 408–428.

Clark, MS and Mills, J 1979, 'Interpersonal attraction in exchange and communal relationships', *Journal of Personality and Social Psychology*, vol. 37, no. 1, pp. 12-24.

Collins, NL and Miller, LC 1994, 'Self-disclosure and liking: A meta-analytic review', *Psychological Bulletin*, vol. 116, no. 3, pp. 457–475.

Derrida, J 1987, 'Women in the beehive: A seminar with Jacques Derrida', trans. J Adner, in A Jardine and P Smith (eds), *Men in feminism*, Methuen, New York, NY, pp. 189–203.

Donath, J and boyd, d 2004, 'Public displays of connection', *BT Technology Journal*, vol. 22, no. 4, pp. 71–82.

Fitzsimmons, J 1985, 'Consumer participation and productivity in service operations', *Interfaces*, vol. 15, pp. 60–67.

Foa, EB and Foa, UG 2012, 'Resource theory of social exchange', in K Törnblom and A Kazemi (eds), *Handbook of social resource theory: Theoretical extensions, empirical insights, and social applications, critical issues in social justice*, Springer, New York, NY, pp. 15–33.

Godbout, J and Caillé, A 1992, *The world of the gift*, McGill-Queen's University Press, Quebéc.

Goffman, E 1971, *Relations in public: Microstudies of the public order*, Allen Lane, London.

Gouldner, AW 1960, 'The norm of reciprocity: A preliminary statement', *American Sociological Review*, vol. 25, no. 2, pp. 161–178.

Gudeman, S 2001, *The anthropology of economy: Community, market, and culture*, Blackwell, Oxford.

Homans, GC 1958, 'Social behavior as exchange', *American Journal of Sociology*, vol. 63, no. 6, pp. 597-606.

Humphreys, A and Grayson, K 2008, 'The intersecting roles of consumer and producer: A critical perspective on co-production, co-creation and prosumption', *Sociological Compass*, vol. 2, pp. 963–980.

Hyde, L 1983, *The gift: Imagination and the erotic life of property*, Vintage Books, New York, NY.

Jenkins, H 1992, *Textual poachers: Television fans and participatory culture*, Routledge, New York, NY and London.

Jenkins, H, Ford, S and Green, J 2013, *Spreadable media: Creating value and meaning in a networked culture*, New York University Press, New York, NY.

John, NA 2017, *The age of sharing*, John Wiley & Sons, London.

Katz, J, Rice, R, Acord, S, Dasgupta, K and David, K 2004, 'Personal mediated communication and the concept of community in theory and practice', in P Kalbfleisch (ed), *Communication and community, communication yearbook*, vol. 28, Erlbaum, Mahwah, NJ, pp. 315–371.

Kennedy, J 2013, 'Rhetorics of sharing: Data, imagination and desire', in G Lovink and M Rasch (eds), *Unlike US reader: Social media monopolies and their alternatives*, no. 8, Institute of Network Cultures, Amsterdam, pp. 127–136.

Klamer, A 2003, 'Gift economy', in R Towse (ed), *A handbook of cultural economics*, Edward Elgar Publishing, Cheltenham, pp. 241–247.

Lamberton, C and Rose, R 2012, 'When is ours better than mine? A framework for understanding and altering participation in commercial sharing systems', *Journal of Marketing*, vol. 76, pp. 109–125.

Lanier, C Jr. and Schau, H 2007, 'Culture and co-creation: Exploring consumers' inspirations and aspirations for writing and posting on-line fan fiction' in R Belk, and J Sherry Jr. (eds), *Consumer culture theory: Research in consumer behavior*, vol. 11, Elsevier, Amsterdam, pp. 321–342.

Latour, B 2007, *Reassembling the social: An introduction to actor-network-theory*, Oxford University Press, Oxford.

Leadbeater, C 2008, *We-think: Mass innovation, not mass production*, Profile Books, London.

Leadbeater, C and Miller, P 2004, *The pro-am revolution: How enthusiasts are changing our economy and society*, Demos, London.

Lerner, RM, Skinner, EA and Sorell, GT 1980, 'Methodological implications of contextual/dialectic theories of development', *Human Development*, vol. 23, no. 4, pp. 225–235.

Liebowitz, SJ 2006, 'File sharing: Creative destruction or just plain destruction?', *Journal of Law and Economics*, vol. 49, no. 1, pp. 1-28.

Marti, S and Garcia-Molina, H 2003, 'Identity crisis: Anonymity vs reputation in P2P systems', *P2P 2003 proceedings, IEEE*, pp. 134–141.

Martin, J and Harder, JW 1994, 'Bread and roses: Justice and the distribution of financial and socioemotional rewards in organizations', *Social Justice Research*, vol. 7, pp. 241–264.

Mauss, M 1954, *The gift: The form and reason for exchange in archaic societies*, Psychology Press, London.

Meikle, G 2014, 'Inaugural lecture: Sharing and social media', *University of Westminster*, viewed 30 April 2019, <www.youtube.com/watch?v=kuS8TDbjp_A>.

Molm, LD 2003, 'Theoretical comparisons of forms of exchange', *Sociological Theory*, vol. 21, no. 1, pp. 1-17.

Moore, GE 2004, *Principia Ethica*, Dover Publications, Mineola.

Murstein, BI, Cerreto, M and MacDonald, MG 1977, 'A theory and investigation of the effect of exchange-orientation on marriage and friendship', *Journal of Marriage and the Family*, vol. 39, no. 3, pp. 543-548.

Parry, J 1986, 'The gift, the Indian gift and the "Indian gift"', *Man*, vol. 21, no. 3, pp. 453–473.

Polanyi, K 1944, *The great transformation*, Rinehart & Company, Inc., New York and Toronto.

Postigo, H 2003, 'Emerging sources of labor on the internet: The case of America Online volunteers', *International Review of Social History*, vol. 48, pp. 205–223.

Preece, J 2000, *Online communities: Designing usability, supporting sociability*, John Wiley & Sons Ltd, New York, NY.

Reagle, JM 2010, *Good faith collaboration: The culture of wikipedia*, MIT Press, Cambridge, MA.

Rheingold, H 1993, *The virtual community: Homesteading on the electronic frontier*, Basic Books, Cambridge.

Rheingold, H 2002, *Smart mobs: The next social revolution*, Basic Books, New York, NY.

Rousseau, DM and Schalk, R 2000, 'Learning from cross-national perspectives on psychological contracts', in DM Rousseau and R Schalk (eds), *Psychological contracts in employment: Cross-national perspectives*, Sage Publications, Inc., Thousand Oaks, CA, pp. 283-302.

Sahlins, M 1972, *Stone age economics*, Aldine-Atherton, Chicago, IL.

Sherry, JF 1983, 'Gift giving in anthropological perspective', *Journal of Consumer Research*, vol. 10, no. 2, pp. 157–168.

Shore, LM and Coyle-Shapiro, JA-M 2003, 'New developments in the employee-organization relationship', *Journal of Organizational Behavior*, vol. 24, pp. 443-450.

Shirky, C 2008, *Here comes everybody: The power of organizing without organizations*, Penguin, New York, NY.

Skågeby, J 2008, *Gifting technologies: Ethnographic studies of end-users and social media sharing*, PhD thesis, Linköping University, Sweden.

Stalder, F and Sützl, W (eds) 2011, 'Ethics of sharing', Special issue of *International Review of Information Ethics*, vol. 15, no. 9.

Stallman, R 2009, 'Ending the war on sharing', *Richard Stallman's personal site*, viewed 17 March 2014, <http://stallman.org/articles/end-war-on-sharing.html>.

Tapscott, D and Williams, AD 2008, *Wikinomics: How mass collaboration changes everything*, Portfolio, New York, NY.

Thibaut, JW and Kelley, HH 1959, *The social psychology of groups*, John Wiley & Sons, New York, NY.

Turkle, S 2011, *Alone together: Why we expect more from technology and less from each other*, Basic Books, New York, NY.

Van Dijck, J 2013, *The culture of connectivity: A critical history of social media*, Oxford University Press, Oxford and New York, NY.

von Hippel, E 2005, *Democratizing innovation*, MIT Press, Cambridge, MA and London.

Weber, S 2004, *The success of open source*, Harvard University Press, Cambridge, MA and London.

Wesch, M 2009, 'YouTube and you: Experiences of self-awareness in the context collapse of the recording webcam', *Explorations in Media Ecology*, vol. 8, no. 2, pp. 19–34.

Wittel, A 2011, 'Qualities of sharing and their transformations in the digital age', *International Review of Information Ethics*, vol. 15, no. 9, pp. 3–8.

3   Practice-Centred Approaches to Sharing

Introduction

This chapter shows how there is slippage both in how sharing is framed theoretically, in relation to gift-giving, exchange and reciprocity, and in terms of how sharing is configured as an economic, distributive and social practice. Practice-based approaches can develop these distinct understandings of sharing further.

Without an agreed definition of sharing, many scholars have found it useful to frame sharing through practice approaches (Kelty 2008; Lankshear and Knobel 2010; Bräuchler and Postill 2010; Spaargaren, Weenink and Lamers 2016) and to use practices as the basis from which to analyse more broadly what is it people do in relation to media (Postill 2010; Couldry 2012). Practice-theoretical approaches ask, '[W]hat, quite simply, are people doing in relation to media across a whole range of situations and contexts?' (Couldry 2012, p. 39). After describing briefly what practice-theoretical approaches entail I then consider the key elements of practices—which I describe as competencies (including knowledge and techniques), materiality and symbolic values—and show how these are organised as part of everyday practices of sharing.

Intentions of Practice-Based Theories

Social practice theories attempt to understand the dynamic aspects of social life without prescribing agency or structure as the organising force. They emerged across the works of prominent social theory scholars such as Pierre Bourdieu, Michel Foucault (his later works), Marshall Sahlins, Jean-François Lyotard, Charles Taylor, Judith Butler, Harold Garfinkel and Anthony Giddens, although can also be traced to the philosophical work of Martin Heidegger and Ludwig Wittgenstein. Each formulation emphasises that action is always already social and positions practices as *the* unit of analysis. For Taylor,

> meanings and norms implicit in [. . .] practices are not just in the minds of the actors but are out there in the practices themselves,

practices which cannot be conceived as a set of individual actions, but which are essentially modes of social relations, or mutual action.

(1971, p. 27)

This is not to say that there is a cohesive or coherent schema to contemporary practice theories. They constitute a loosely grouped body of literature in which a 'practice approach' is adopted. A common criticism of practice-based literature is that it 'fails to make clear just what social practices are' (Barnes 2001, p. 26).

Rather, a practice is an *entity*, a nexus point of interrelated elements, and a *performance*, which presupposes practice and constitutes practice as entity (Schatzki 1996). For Southerton et al.,

[t]he relationship between practices and performances is recursive: practices configure performances, and practices are reproduced, and stabilised, adapted and innovated, through performances.

(2012, p. 240)

Sharing as a performance is a momentary nexus of constitutive elements that both practitioner and observer recognise as sharing. Sharing as an entity emerges and is recognised through the repeated performance of sharing practices in generally cohesive ways. Performances of sharing both constitute sharing as an entity and presuppose sharing as a practice.

Descriptions and Distinctions of Practices

In an early philosophical approach to social practices, Theodore Schatzki (1996) describes a practice as a '"bundle" of activities' (p. 71) or elements 'packaged' together to form a particular 'nexus of doings and sayings' (p. 89). However, there are variations in exactly what is understood to constitute the elements, or the doings and sayings, of a practice. For example, Schatzki (1996) goes on to further define a practice as understandings of 'what to say and do'; rules, including 'principles, precepts and instructions'; and '"teleoaffective" structures embracing ends, projects, tasks, purposes, beliefs, emotions and moods' (p. 89), which 'organise' the practice (p. 99). He later distinguishes among practical understandings, the capacity to know what to do and how to carry out actions and general understandings, which are shared common understandings such as the cultural imaginary (Schatzki 2002). Similarly, Andreas Reckwitz (2002) introduces the distinction between *Praxis*, which in German means social activity as a whole, and *Praktik*, a routinised behaviour (p. 249). Reckwitz also argues that practices are composed of a set of interconnected elements; however he identifies these as 'forms of bodily activities, forms of mental activities, 'things' and their use, a background knowledge in the form of understanding, know-how, states of emotion and motivational knowledge' (2002, p. 249). Reckwitz locates these elements as the site through which practices are recognizable to both practitioners and observers with appropriate cultural knowledge. Importantly, Reckwitz introduces a focus on materiality: 'things' and their use.

Perhaps one reason practice theorists have not agreed upon a categorical set of elements is because practices are at once actualised and abstract. For consumption theorist Alan Warde (2005), '[a]s general theories of practice they tend to be idealised, abstract and insufficiently attentive to the social processes involved in the creation and reproduction of practices' (p. 135). It is difficult to reduce practices to a distinct set of elements that can be methodically applied across diverse phenomena. Yet that has not stopped practice theorists—and those who seek to apply practice-based theories to their own field of studies, such as I—from attempting to converge on a concrete set of practice elements.

Even within specific fields of study, there are disagreements on what constitutes practices. A large body of work on social practices has emerged in consumption studies. Drawing on Schatzki (1996, p. 89), Warde (2005) consolidates practice components into '(1) understandings, (2) procedures and (3) engagements' (p. 134). Elizabeth Shove, Mika Pantzar and Matt Watson (2012) expand upon their own conceptualisations of practice theory in *The Dynamics of Social Practice: Everyday Life and How it Changes*, which draws on Actor Network Theory and science and technology studies to consider a 'materialised theory of practice' (p. 10). In their discussion of a wide range of consumption-oriented practices, Shove, Pantzar and Watson define practice elements as materials, 'including things, technologies, tangible physical entities, and the stuff of which objects are made' (Shove et al. 2012, p. 14); competencies, 'which encompass skill, know-how and technique' (Ibid.); and meanings—which includes 'symbolic meanings, ideas and aspirations' (Ibid).

Southerton et al. (2012) similarly distil practices into three specific elements: 'material objects' which I take to include all goods or resources that can be shared, whether material or immaterial (the 'what'); 'practical know how', the knowledge and discourses around conventions of sharing as well as the enactment or 'doing' of sharing; and 'socially sanctioned objectives', the motivations, desires and impetuses for sharing that are incorporated into or drawn from the cultural imaginary:

> When operationalised, practices are generally treated as configurations of recognizable, intelligible and describable elements which comprise their conditions of existence. While there is no single agreed typology of elements [. . .] some combination of material objects, practical know how, and socially sanctioned objectives is deployed, these often in context of socio-technical systems, social and economic institutions, and modes of spatial and temporal organization. Such

elements both configure how practices are performed and make them identifiable to practitioners and non-practitioners alike.

(2012, p. 240)

In social practice theory literature, meanings and understandings are commonly conflated and generally conceived as part of the same category. Competencies are understood as being more practical, such as bodily 'skills' and 'know-how' rather than mental activities. There are degrees of overlap, especially between competencies and symbolic values, and others may categorise elements differently or more loosely. In the following descriptions of sharing practices, I use the categories of symbolic values, materiality and competencies.

Sharing Practices

In media studies, practice approaches are not new but follow a tradition of studying domestic practices in relation to media technologies (Silverstone, Hirsch and Morley 1992; Silverstone 1994; Mackay and Ivey 2004; Bakardjieva 2005). The turn towards practices marks a shift in the critical language of media research, although it has not been universally embraced. For instance, Mark Hobart (2010) quips, '[H]as not the phrase 'media practices' been used so promiscuously as to be a cliché?' (p. 55).

Oriented towards an educational function, Colin Lankshear and Michele Knobel (2010) clearly state a practice-theoretical approach when providing the thematic and contextual background to their edited collection *DIY Media: Creating, Sharing and Learning with New Technologies*, which contains contributions addressing a range of do-it-yourself media practices such as podcasting:

> Podcasting . . . involves using particular kinds of tools, techniques and technologies to achieve the goals and purposes that podcasters aim to achieve, and to use them in the ways that people known as podcasters recognise as appropriate to their endeavour in terms of their goals and values.
>
> (Lankshear and Knobel 2010, pp. 1–2)

Although neither critical nor reflexive, Lankshear and Knobel identify the range of elements their practice approach is concerned with. These include cultural knowledge, tools and skills, means of recognising and intentions of doing and being. While Lankshear and Knobel state a practice-centred approach, they do not gesture towards the work of early and emerging practice theorists who sought to establish a terminological and theoretical framework.

Acknowledging the contribution of practice theorists, Nick Couldry (2012) details many practices that exemplify digital culture, such as 'searching and search-enabling', 'showing and being shown', 'presencing', 'archiving' and 'complex' media practices: 'keeping up with the news', 'commentary', 'keeping all channels open' and 'screening out'. Although this typology of media practices is 'initial, if crude' (p. 44), the omission of sharing as a distinct practice is symptomatic of digital culture critiques where sharing is acknowledged but rarely probed.

Practices may be both 'media-related' (Hobart 2010) and 'media-oriented, in all its looseness and openness' (Couldry 2010, p. 39). By this I mean that there is a tension between sharing as it is implied through 'recognised, complex forms of social activity and articulation, through which agents set out to maintain or change themselves, others and the world around them under varying conditions' (Hobart 2010, p. 63) and as it is defined within 'bounded worlds of media organisation' (Postill 2010, p. 20). Such tensions call into question issues of power, in terms of who regulates and sanctions practices in the field. Cammaerts (2011) describes three particular arrangements of sharing practices in digital culture with distinct power and symbolic processes: sharing code, sharing content and sharing access. He argues that each form of sharing co-opts and appropriates capitalist agendas. Sharing code diverts revenue processes to indirect or auxiliary services rather than bypasses commodity markets entirely. Sharing content, described here as 'propriety software, music, e-books, magazines, films, TV shows and even live sport broadcasts' (p. 52), disrupts property rights regimes yet problematically supports intrusive advertising or premium downloading services. In each of these arrangements, the object shared (code, content, access) has potential market value. This is distinct to the mostly affective content described in my empirical data.

In recent years there has been a growth in critical attention to the conceptualisation and mobilisation of sharing in digital contexts. In particular, Andreas Wittel, Russell Belk and Nicholas John each demonstrate an understanding of sharing and the significance of sharing in everyday mediated practices. These scholars engage explicitly with the concept of sharing in digital contexts but not fully with what people do when they are sharing. Additionally, there are others who balance a critical perspective on digital platforms with their imperatives to 'share' with an understanding of the reasons users enjoy using such services (see Meikle 2016; Cammaerts 2011).

There is also a larger group of scholars who pay attention to specific practices of sharing on social media platforms and other online networks. This group range widely in terms of their scholarly fields. Their work commonly reprises existing theories of exchange, public goods, reciprocity and gift-giving to describe sharing. This work is exemplified in the work of Jörgen Skågeby (2008), Nancy Baym (2011) and Jose van Dijck (2013). It is also pertinent to point to those engaged in studies of the emergence and practices of media-sharing communities (e.g., see Burgess and Green 2018; Jenkins, Ford and Green 2013) and economic frameworks (see Benkler 2004; Botsman and Rogers 2010).

The *how* of sharing is rarely the subject of extensive qualitative analysis, although there are several qualitative studies, which address sharing practices as they relate to other social phenomena. For example, while not explicitly adopting a practice-based approach, Andrea Baker (2012) looks at how rock music fans coordinating the exchange of material culture through mediated communication strengthens bonds within the community and how social status is accrued through the provision of resources, including information. Similarly, Jessa Lingel and Mor Naaman (2012) look at how videos of music concerts are later shared via YouTube to address the use of technology in social settings and how technologies carry implications for the construction of labour. Such studies contribute to understandings of how sharing is an integral part of digital culture, but more is required to illuminate the social significance of sharing for participants. That there are few qualitative studies of sharing is the precise gap that this book seeks to address.

A Theory of Sharing Practice

In the remainder of this book, I draw on data from a qualitative study of everyday uses of social media platforms and other online networks. I use these data to extend the conceptual framework of sharing. The qualitative data provide rich accounts of sharing practices and perception of sharing norms. One such example of the sorts of discussion that emerged follows:

> I think the concept of sharing is a difficult concept. How do you define it? I would sort of define it as giving away a little of what you have or receiving a little bit of something that somebody else has. And I have an idea that these types of sharing are actually adding to what you have so it's not the same type of sharing. I mean if you share your ideas then you'll actually get more ideas so I think it's a different type of sharing don't you think? I think also that it is free, maybe that's what comes in when you talk about this type of media sharing which is always something that I have found really interesting. Because it's free, it's easy to give away because you're not actually giving it away. I think the real sharing is when you have less afterwards. So why would you do it? You do it because there is some perceived thing that you get out of it as well. Otherwise people wouldn't get into it. It's not really something you think about every day.
>
> (Katja)

Katja is a 28-year-old freelance photographer originally from Germany now living in Melbourne with her boyfriend, who is himself from Brazil. A highly competent communication technology user, she spends a great portion of most days on social media sites and regularly uses communication technologies such as SnapChat, WhatsApp and Face-Time to communicate with friends and family overseas. Katja finds that she has a number of ways of describing sharing: using the language of gift-giving (Mauss 1954), it can be giving something away or receiving something that someone else has given away where the person giving has less; it can be giving something away so that the other person has more but the person giving has no less. Katja also distinguishes between the sharing of material and immaterial objects, such as the sharing of a DVD and the sharing of a digital movie file.

Katja struggles with these different definitions of sharing, highlighting the nature of defining sharing as a type of practice. This difficulty in articulating what constitutes a practice explicitly is consistent with social theories that assume a tacit understanding of practice. For Katja, sharing occurs when an object is redistributed but does not change ownership completely; only 'a little' is given or received. Actions of both giving and receiving are part of the performance of sharing. The reciprocation of the object giving is necessary for the giving to be performed and vice versa. Sharing for Katja has an expectation of some form of reciprocation, although she does not identify the necessity of a direct exchange. Instead, where objects are redistributed or gifted, reciprocation comes through what she describes as 'some perceived thing that you get out of it' which may be satisfaction of the deed or gratitude. Katja also does not identify a time frame in terms of cycles of giving and receiving within her framework of sharing. The giving is not performed in response to a previously gifted object or in expectation of a later return in kind, such as a social debt.

There are notable tensions within Katja's understanding of sharing. Indeed, the quote is provided earlier at length because it evocatively illustrates such tensions. First, she describes sharing through a framework of gift-giving, drawing on the cultural imaginary of generosity and sacrifice (Taylor 2002), which she describes as 'giving away a little'; mythologies of gift-giving (Hyde 1983), 'there is some perceived thing that you get out of it'; and moral norms of how one ought to behave (Gouldner 1960), 'the real sharing is when you have less afterwards', which conflict with her own means of doing sharing, specifically when sharing media files.

Katja is a useful introduction to the qualitative data, as she demonstrates the ambiguity and complexity many participants described with regard to their sharing practices. In the next sections of this chapter, I use the qualitative data to illustrate how sharing practices are understood in terms of symbolic values, materiality and competencies in everyday life in relation to digital media.

Symbolic Values

Sharing practices are socially situated and enact values of community. People typically associate feelings of satisfaction and worth, or feelings of generosity and gratitude, with sharing. These values describe particular desires and 'ends', which Andreas Reckwitz (2012) calls 'affective intensities', in sharing practices. Symbolic values are routinised in 'recognisable patterns' (Reckwitz 2012, p. 251). Specifically, symbolic values capture the motivation of sharing practices which is to *effect social intensification* (Wittel 2011) and build community. Social intensification endures across specific performances of sharing.

Within the thick descriptions of the data there are examples of know-how about the symbolic values of sharing. One participant. Darryl, a 32-year-old software developer, describes sharing as 'important', 'interesting', 'valuable' and 'material'. Darryl is university-educated and full-time employed. He is very social, belongs to a sports team, and is a regular attendee at supper clubs (social media coordinated groups who meet to eat out at different restaurants), where he is particularly hopeful of meeting a romantic partner. He is also active on online dating apps. Darryl associates feelings of satisfaction and worth with sharing, while Katja associates feelings of generosity and gratitude with sharing. Katja and Darryl describe such effects of social intensification within their performance of sharing, which is, in turn, embedded within their perceived understanding of sharing practice.

Performances of sharing enact values of social intensification. For example, Philip, a 27-year-old DJ, notes that how he goes about sharing music both speaks to media specificity and illustrates how his sharing effects social intensification with others. While an undergrad, Philip used to be a regular DJ at an electronica music night in a local bar; over the years he got to know many of the regular attendees, became Facebook friends with them and met them at other music events. Now forging a career in games development, he has less time for DJing but still spends a great deal of time perusing and enjoying music. No longer DJing regularly, he still likes to share his musical discoveries with friends. Speaking on how he does this, he says,

> We could very easily just copy our entire [music] collections onto USB sticks and pass them around amongst each other. . . . But aside from running into complications around copyright and ideas like that there's something less personal about these massive transfers of information rather than this notion of picking out a particular song or video or snippet that you think might be of personal interest to somebody and then just sharing that one thing. I see it sort of like the difference between making somebody a handmade gift and buying them a gift card to some arbitrary store.
>
> (Philip)

While the same object can be shared in many different ways, Philip selects the method appropriate for the relationship he has with the person he is sharing with or, more specifically, the value he places on that relationship. While sharing his entire music collection might seem to be more generous than sharing a single song, it is, in his view, less personal than him taking the time to select a particular song that he thinks the other person will enjoy. He is not only demonstrating his value of the relationship but is also demonstrating his understanding of that person based on his knowledge of them. The value is shown through the labour of selection rather than the value of the digital media object. Philip's actions are socially intelligible without being explicitly explained. The sharing of music is embedded within Philip's ongoing social practices in which he shares his interests with friends and is part of broader and more complex social negotiations embedded in everyday life.

Another participant, Vanessa—a 29-year-old university lecturer—shares media files amongst her peers. Vanessa described herself as very gregarious, with a great deal of overlap between her personal and professional life. Her evenings and weekends were often spent socialising with colleagues. Talking about the types of objects shared, Vanessa said, 'Torrented files, plenty of those. I share torrented files on an external hard drive, which seems to be routinely passed around my friends'. Vanessa, like Philip, gets pleasure out of distributing her resources to others. Unlike Philip, she does not seek to specify which file goes to which person. The hard drive (as an established media form still much in use) acts as a carrier of value and meaning and as a material presence in her friendships. It circulates outside of her immediate control (though she can easily retrieve it by simply asking for it back), reinforcing her relational ties amongst a group of people. For Vanessa, distributing torrented files on an external hard drive is the most logical means of sharing these objects. The physicality of the portable hard drive may also limit whom she can share them with too. Vanessa's torrented files generally go to the friends she sees most regularly. These are usually work friends she says, 'because they're the ones who are around'. As Vanessa's example demonstrates, people participate in sharing practices by 'reacting' to social situations in ways that make sense for them to do so. For Vanessa, the openness with which she shares her acquired files is more meaningful to her than concern about perceptions of the legality of how she acquired them.

Sharing effects social intensification by tracing connections from one person to another. A USB or hard drive containing media files passed around an office space or group of friends saves unnecessary data downloads. It also reinforces ties within a group, for the files are unequivocally distributed amongst each member. Group members might be able to ascertain, based on their understanding of one another's tastes, who uploaded particular movies or media to the circulated drive. The device serves as a symbol of connectivity. The hard drive may pass through many sets of hands. It might be carefully guarded, password-protected and handed only to select people, or it might be passed across groups through common members. Sharing objects shows where boundaries exist in social networks (Malinowski 1922) and the parameters of community.

The relation of symbolic values to the materiality and competencies of sharing shift according to sociocultural and temporal contexts. What makes sense in one context may not make sense in another. For instance, Katja experienced a shift in her ways of doing and understanding sharing through cultural differentiation when she moved to Australia from overseas:

> Here [in Melbourne] everybody knows that you can't invite all your friends out to dinner to a nice restaurant. You just couldn't do it. People assume the fact that everybody is going to cover their own bill. In Malaysia it's not like that at all. People are a lot more easygoing when it comes to finances.
>
> (Katja)

Katja compares the relationship of sharing practices to perceptions of generosity and social status in Melbourne to Malaysia. Specifically, she demonstrates how different cultures and financial markets affect what sharing practices might be expected to be performed, showing how practices are also understood in relation to other practices. Performances of sharing can demonstrate taste, perform self, enact relationships between subjects and objects and effect social intensification through interconnection with other social practices. Sharing's interconnection with other social practices contributes to the complexity of isolating and describing sharing.

Materiality

The materiality of sharing is already indicated in the descriptions from the earlier data. Materiality plays a constitutive role in sharing practice. The materiality of sharing includes the significance of objects shared (e.g. Miller and Tilley 1996; Appadurai 1986), the material forms and affordances of objects, the social aspects of technology (e.g. Ingold 2000; Latour 2007; Carey 1989; Silverstone and Hirsch 1992), as well as the 'technological underpinnings of culture' (Vannini 2009, p. 3). Everyday life in a networked culture incorporates a whole range of devices across which participants move with varying degrees of fluidity. This notion of foregrounding materiality and inseparability informs my theory of sharing. As Schatzki (2001) argues, 'understanding specific practices always involves apprehending material configurations' (p. 12). Socially coordinated configurations of sharing are often recognised and located by the materiality of that which is being shared, such as digital files in file sharing; affect in social media; or commodities in collaborative consumption (Botsman and Rogers 2010). Sharing is also recognisable by the way in which objects are shared.

Within sharing practice, how objects can be shared is specific to materiality. The way objects are shared and the objects themselves do not constitute sharing; rather, it is only in the interconnection of all the elements that sharing is constituted. I identify three distinct ways of sharing objects.

Objects Can Be Duplicated

Prevalent in the cultural imaginary is the idea that objects being given or received constitute sharing. The process of sharing and the process of giving are very similar and can each be oriented towards the same ends of social intensification. When giving, an object passes from ownership of one person into ownership of another so that the person giving is no longer in ownership of the object or its replica. This type of sharing involves an extension of control rather than transferral of ownership.

Sharing does not mean giving away. Sharing can convey that both parties have what is being shared (time, objects, ideas, etc.), even if not both at the same time. Objects are conveyed from one person to another when they are shared. Sharing requires a receiver but does not require that the receiver respond or reciprocate. When immaterial objects are given, they are not reduced in any way for the person giving, except in the value of scarcity. For example, when participants post on social media, they are sharing their feelings, yet doing so does not reduce those feelings for them. Similarly, when another participant emails a relative a link to a new recipe, he or she is not subsequently without it.

Objects Can Be Divided and Apportioned

An established early lesson of sociability is the sharing of toys or sweets, which indicates that objects can be divided or portioned out. When participants talk about giving or receiving a little of something as sharing, they mean objects that can be divided up and apportioned. Such objects have particular material limitations in that their smallest divisible amount or the available quantity is finite. When shared, the person giving is left with a smaller portion. Objects are not necessarily shared fairly or evenly, although there might be expectations that particular objects under particular social contexts ought to be shared evenly. Social intensification is not necessarily attributable to the evenness of apportioning.

Access to Objects Can Be Shared

Sharing does not always mean duplication or division. Objects can be shared temporarily or temporally. Sharing objects that cannot be duplicated or divided requires sharing access to those objects. Access is specific to the materiality of the object. The sharing of objects requires negotiation, either implicitly or explicitly. Sharing an object does not necessitate sharing ownership of that object. Collaborative consumption is a particular socially coordinated entity of sharing which involves the sharing of access to objects with objectives of community development and social intensification. Objects to which access is shared are typically material, although there are exceptions. For example, many participants share their Wi-Fi passwords with friends and family when they visit their home.

Considerations of Materiality

There are other factors to take into consideration regarding the materiality of sharing practices. As already mentioned, objects to be shared can be immaterial. Ideas, emotions, and knowledge are examples of immaterial objects. For immaterial objects, matters of division are complex. Ownership and access are also multiplied once the object has been shared because sharing also redefines ownership of the object and control of access to it. Sharing an immaterial object is non-reductive; there is not less of the object once it has been shared. Access to the object is no longer in total control of the giver; that control is shared with the recipient at the time of sharing the object, although there may be social rules around how that control may be exercised.

Digital ephemera are significant immaterial objects in a networked culture. While the objects themselves may not be perceived as having material properties, they are afforded by objects that are material—hardware, software and other media devices—which render them able to be encountered.

Ways of thinking about objects to be shared include thinking about the specific material configurations through which the sharing of such objects is afforded. Sharing movies requires that the movie media file be stored on a piece of hardware: a memory stick, a hard drive or server. To access the media file further hardware is required: a smartphone, a tablet, a laptop, a desktop with a monitor or television which if not integrated is attached by HDMI cables or AVI leads, these devices may also require external speakers. Additionally, these devices require operating systems and software that can decode the movie file and present it in the correct format (not to mention infrastructure such as internet connections and a power source). Other media formats such as emails, images and documents require similar configurations in order to be shared.

Sharing practices are influenced by the sociocultural construction of technology and perception of affordances. Attending to the materiality of elements that constitute sharing in everyday life requires the know-how of the material properties of the object and material affordances required to share the object and know-how of the *type* of object.

Types of Objects That Can Be Shared

Objects can be classified by type, and some types of object are more suitable for sharing than others. Each category of object has particular properties of materiality that intersect with competencies of sharing and symbolic values in specific ways.

In defining types of objects, a useful starting point is Foa and Foa's (2012) typology of objects that are exchanged. Their typology consists of six objects, each with distinct properties: services, goods, money, information, status and love (pp. 16–17), definitions of which follow:

> Services: labour, including any activities that 'affect the body or belong- ings of a person'
> Goods: 'material products, objects or materials'
> Money: 'any coin, currency, or token' which has a 'currency of exchange'
> Information: 'advice, opinions, instruction, or enlightenment'
> Status: 'an evaluative judgement that conveys prestige, regard, or esteem'
> Love: 'an expression of affectionate regard, warmth, or comfort'
>
> (2012, pp. 16–17)

Some objects are more concrete than others, meaning that they have particular material forms, their value is universal, and they are reduced for self when shared with another person, that is money. Other types of objects are more particularist, meaning that the persons involved and their relationship to one another matter a great deal for the value of the object, that is, Pusheen emojis.

Although concrete objects such as money, goods and services are typically exchanged for compensation, rather than shared, it is not the object *per se* that defines a performance as sharing. Examples of concrete objects being shared abound in discussions of collaborative consumption as a particular socially (and formally) coordinated entity, although sharing of concrete objects occur in more mundane circumstances also. For instance, co-habiting couples share their finances.

Emphasising this point further, Maya—a 46-year-old public administrator—described how she shares relaxation music with a friend of hers who regularly has trouble sleeping. They both belong to a support group for people with mental illness. Over the years the group have amassed a number of objects and resources that are shared amongst members as needed. One such time arose that Maya described to me:

> I got a text from a friend. She wanted to know if I had any CDs that would help her sleep. She told me that she had been feeling depressed and flat because she hadn't been sleeping well . . . I have a library box with books and things to do with depression and anxiety, she wanted me to check that box to see if there was anything in there.
>
> (Maya)

Objects of information may be particular or universal. Information objects are not symbolic objects, nor are they intended to convey affect. Information objects drawn from my empirical data ranged from coordination, such as organising dinner plans, children pick-ups, availabilities, arrival times and attendances; advice or assistance, including feedback on work, instructions on cake baking and advice on relationships; discussions, such as a team meeting about how to proceed with a project, manage a communal project or to come to general consensus as to where to go for lunch; and gossip, such as chat about how the day/week/weekend/special event went, and personal opinions such as dislike of public transport, or attractiveness of a person. Information objects may be exchanged for compensation or shared in expectation of reciprocity. Sharing information is often compounded in more complex social practices, meaning that the performance of sharing is embedded within other socially coordinated entities such as business practices and other such formalised interactions. For example, Darryl values sharing information with his colleagues. He uses Twitter and Slack to share knowledge on the use of particular software applications.

The final two objects in the typology, love and status, are symbolic objects of affect. Objects of affect are particular, meaning that the persons involved and their relationship to one another matter a great deal for the value of the object. Affect does not reduce in the process of sharing. Objects of affect are enacted through the sharing process or may be mobilised through other objects such as gifts.

One type of object that does not fit easily into Foa and Foa's typology is digital ephemera. Digital ephemera do not necessarily advise, give an opinion, instruct or enlighten such information, nor are they themselves concrete or particularist. While digital ephemera are concrete, in that they have particular properties (indicated by the file extension, i.e., .dox, .jpeg, .avi) they are only made concrete through the affordances of other objects. A photo printed on paper has a particular tangibility which affords sharing by physical movement—such as hand to hand—and includes the possibility for its properties to be altered in some way—such as folding, fading or tearing. A digital photo is assumed to reach the other person with the exact properties it was sent with (Gitelman 2004), yet properties of digital media files are also unstable and do not guarantee conditions of reception, that is transcoding. The recipient requires a digital device on which to receive the photo. The device may have alternative decoding software that might render the photo differently; resolutions vary across different monitors and screens which will also affect the reception of the photograph. Neither physical nor digital formats guarantee that the photo's properties will be unchanged in reception. Additionally, devices, hardware and infrastructure limit what digital media can be shared. For example, one participant shares details about films via social media posts rather than actual digital movie files because there are infrastructure limitations and legal and cost prohibitions for sending large digital files to her friends.

Knowledge of how objects can be shared intersects with understandings of the material properties and classification of objects. Furthermore, the material properties of the object do not define a performance as sharing; rather, it is the configuration of materiality together with the effect of social intensification and degree of competence that identifies the performance as sharing.

Competencies

The term *competencies* is drawn from social practices literature (Shove et al. 2012). Constitutive elements of competencies include ways of doing sharing, such as bodily actions, 'know-how' and tacit knowledge about sharing. Know-how relates to motivations or intentions of sharing, feelings around sharing and objects that are shared. There is conflict within know-how in terms of understanding and interpreting sharing. Know-how is drawn on to make sense of action by practitioners and observers, coding particular performances as sharing and others as not sharing.

Ways of doing sharing involve the transferal or extension of ownership of a material, immaterial or affective object from one participant to another. Ways of doing sharing include non-mediated encounters, such as face-to-face, and mediated encounters such as social media, telephone calls, video calls, text messages, instant messages/chat, emails and through distributive interfaces and software. Both mediated and non-mediated ways of doing sharing can be asynchronous, meaning the performance is not time-bound. A key way of doing sharing identified in the data and normative in a networked culture is sharing affective material through personal websites and proprietary social media platforms, through which many people can be shared with simultaneously.

From the examples in the data, the ways of doing sharing can be categorised into Table 3.1.

Practices of sharing include routine, interconnected bodily performances. There are multiple ways of 'doing' sharing, meaning there are multiple formations of bodily actions that can constitute the performance of sharing. Also, ways of doing sharing traverse a range of spatial, temporal and material arrangements. Ways of 'doing' sharing (i.e., face-to-face, phone calls, text, chat, email, social media) represent the movement of the practice, which is distinct to the symbolic value of the performance. Participants make decisions on how to do sharing based on many factors—their location, the accessibility of the other person (their physical location, how their time might be presently occupied, devices and interfaces they might have access to), the suitability of the way of sharing (i.e., sharing a personal story in a Facebook status update rather than a private email) and the means by which the object can be shared, which relates to the materiality of the object to be shared and affordances for sharing. These decisions are made within a continuum of what makes sense for them to do. Decisions are specific to the practice rather than the practitioner.

Table 3.1 Ways of doing sharing

	Synchronous	Asynchronous
Non-mediated	Synchronous non-mediated encounters: participants involved in the encounter are located such that they may interact without the necessity of a communications device. The practice of sharing is usually performed at the same time as it is experienced, e.g., sharing a cab ride.	Asynchronous non-mediated encounters: participants involved in the encounter are located in such a way that the effect of a practice of sharing may be experienced after it has been performed, e.g., sharing a hot desk in a communal workspace.
Mediated	Synchronous mediated encounters: the people involved in the interaction do so synchronously. Each participant occupies a distinct space to the other so that the interaction is mediated through communications devices. The practice of sharing is performed at the same time as it is experienced, e.g., sharing a phone call.	Asynchronous mediated encounters: participants involved in the interaction do so asynchronously, the practice of sharing is experienced at a later time than when it was performed. A single performance of sharing may be experienced by a number of people following its performance for the period in which the performance is accessible, e.g., sharing a blog post.

Configurations of Practice

Practices are subject to standards of acceptability, which are commonly recognisable. Schatzki points to the social processes that coordinate a practice (Warde 2013). Such social processes might include judgements of correctness, formalisation and codification. There are significant contestations between formalisations and codifications of sharing which need be acknowledged. As Warde describes, this recognition frequently takes the form of codification and 'documentation of rules, procedures and standards' (Warde 2013, p. 64). In the case of sharing, formalisation occurs at the level of the social media platform interface, and intellectual property policies and laws of governing bodies. Interfaces literally code sharing by affording certain performances over others. Another form of codification of sharing practice occurs in the popular press with their descriptions of how to share appropriately and vigorous examples of the fall-out of sharing performances that do not conform (evidenced through the regular examples in popular press of oversharing-related catastrophes), or in institutional policy documents which describe which performances are sanctioned and which are not. These types of documentation, together with informal processes of social sanctioning, such as stating 'cool story bro' to an over-indulgent Facebook post, and of social rules forged more intimately among friends, colleagues, and lovers show the presence of judgements of acceptable performances of sharing which formalise and underpin the practice.

Formalisation is a significant process of practice. This is not to say that the codification of practices converges or agrees. Sharing is especially complex in that there are competing attempts to formalise the practice, such as peer-to-peer file-sharing advocates, objectors and collaborative consumption organisations who each attempt to formalise sharing practices through a documentation of rules. Each formalisation emphasises the existence of sharing practice as an entity beyond the mind of the practitioner:

> Some practices are relatively simple to spot in that they are shared, somewhat formalised, descriptions, prescriptions and definitions of proper performance . . . [with] a readily observable trail of relatively unambiguous indicators—documents, rules and guides—demonstrating that a practice is 'out there', existing across space and time, and figuring as a recognisable entity that people can join, defect from or resist.
>
> (Shove and Spurling 2013, p. 32)

Specific configurations of elements are recognisable as particular formalisations. There are many configurations that compose sharing practice: file sharing, social media sharing, commons/open source and collaborative consumption. Each function with specific regulations and social sanctions, but overall may still be identified as sharing by practitioners and observers. Practitioners may carry know-how of certain configurations and not others. There are also distinctions between practitioners carrying particular configurations of sharing practice: 'different agents carry out different arrays of activities at different field stations with varying degrees of commitment, embodied skill and publicness' (Postill 2010, pp. 16–17). Acknowledging different configurations and capacities for carrying practice allows for a more nuanced account of sharing. Configurations are the formalisation of specific dynamics of elements of sharing practice. Configurations overlap and emerge at different times, with sufficient consistency that they are recognisable to practitioners and observers. Because of this, practices are not static but are dynamic processes of transformation and stability (Shove et al. 2012).

A Theory of Sharing

Sharing practices have distinct boundaries that are persistent and recognisable. It is important to restate that these practices are constituted through the intersections of these elements and that the co-constitutive relations of these elements to each other are specific to sharing.

The theory of sharing put forward in this book is summarised in Table 3.2.

Each practice has a distinct relationship between elements. With sharing, symbolic values are the most readily identified element of the practice, with little change over contexts; for example, since Malinowski's study of Trobriand culture (1922) it has been identified that sharing is motivated by social intensification. Types of object and modalities of sharing objects are also relatively static; however, the development of networked culture has afforded new ways of sharing objects and at a greater scale. Competencies are the most dynamic element of sharing practice. This is evidenced by evolving norms and efforts towards formalisation and codification. Because of these dynamic processes, sharing practices cannot be identified or defined by competencies alone.

This chapter characterises the key elements of sharing practices and their arrangements. It has set out the categorical elements by which sharing can be documented and recognised as a practice. Sharing practices can be recognised by the configuration of symbolic values, materiality and competencies. Symbolic values incorporate the motivations and aspirations of sharing practices, such as those that are 'socially sanctioned' (Southerton et al. 2012), as well as significance and affect, and the desired 'ends' of sharing. Materiality acknowledges the material phenomena through which the social exists, the materiality of objects, arrangements and flows. It also acknowledges that immaterial objects are realised through material matter. I use the term *objects* comprehensively to include material objects as well as both immaterial objects and affective objects, such as digital ephemera, thoughts and emotions. Competencies refer to the multiple forms of understandings, know-how, implicit and explicit rules, norms, skills, techniques, conventions and embodied knowledge of sharing.

Table 3.2 A theory of sharing practice

SYMBOLIC VALUES	MATERIALITY	COMPETENCIES
All sharing effects social intensification, or desires to build community. Reception is a necessary condition for social intensification.	There are three modalities of sharing objects: Objects can be duplicated. ➡ Objects can be divided and apportioned. Access to objects can be shared.	Sharing involves an extension of control of an object. Know-how about such actions may be explicit or tacit. Norms around how control is extended are continually evolving relative to context and in concurrence with efforts towards formalisation by parties with intentions of gains.

References

Appadurai, A 1986, 'Introduction: Commodities and the politics of value', in A Appadurai (ed), *The social life of things: Commodities in cultural perspective*, Cambridge University Press, Cambridge, MA, pp. 3–63.

Bakardjieva, M 2005, *Internet society: The internet in everyday life*, Sage, London and Thousand Oaks, CA.

Baker, A 2012, 'The exchange of material culture among rock fans in online communities, *Information, Communication & Society*, vol. 15, no. 4, pp. 519–536.

Barnes, B 2001, 'Practice as collective action', in TR Schatzki, K Knorr-Cetina and E von Savigny (eds), *The practice turn in contemporary theory*, Routledge, London and New York, NY, pp. 17–28.

Baym, N 2011, 'The Swedish model: Balancing markets and gifts in the music industry', *Popular Communication*, vol. 9, no. 1, pp. 22–38.

Benkler, Y 2004, 'Sharing nicely: On shareable goods and the emergence of sharing as a modality of economic production', *The Yale Law Journal*, vol. 114, no. 2, pp. 273–358.

Botsman, R and Rogers, R 2010, *What's mine is yours: The rise of collaborative consumption*, HarperCollins, New York, NY.

Bräuchler, B and Postill, J (eds) 2010, *Theorising media and practice*, Berghahn Books, Oxford and New York, NY.

Burgess, J and Green, J 2018, *YouTube: Online video and participatory culture*, 2nd edition, John Wiley & Sons, Lanham, MD.

Cammaerts, B 2011, 'Disruptive sharing in a digital age: Rejecting neoliberalism?', *Continuum: Journal of Media & Cultural Studies*, vol. 25, no. 1, pp. 47–62.

Carey, J 1989, *Communication as culture*, Unwin-Hyman, Boston, MA.

Couldry, N 2012, *Media, society, world: Social theory and digital media practice*, Polity, London.

Foa, EB and Foa, UG 2012, 'Resource theory of social exchange', in K Törnblom and A Kazemi (eds), *Handbook of social resource theory: Theoretical extensions, empirical insights, and social applications, critical issues in social justice*, Springer, New York, NY, pp. 15–33.

Gitelman, L 2004, 'Media, materiality, and the measure of the digital; or, the case of sheet music and the problem of piano rolls', in L Rabinovitz and A Geil (eds), *Memory bytes: History, technology, and digital culture*, Duke University Press, Durham, NC, pp. 199–217.

Gouldner, AW 1960, 'The norm of reciprocity: A preliminary statement', *American Sociological Review*, vol. 25, pp. 161–178.

Hobart, M 2010, 'What do we mean by "media practices?"', in B Bräuchler and J Postill (eds), *Theorising media and practice*, Berghahn Books, Oxford and New York, NY, pp. 55–76.

Hyde, L 1983, *The gift: Imagination and the erotic life of property*, Vintage Books, New York, NY.

Ingold, T 2000, *The perception of the environment: Essays on livelihood, dwelling and skill*, Routledge, London and New York, NY.

Jenkins, H, Ford, S and Green, J 2013, *Spreadable media: Creating value and meaning in a networked culture*, New York University Press, New York, NY.

Kelty, C 2008, *Two bits: The cultural significance of free software*, Duke University Press, Durham, NC and London.

Lankshear, C and Knobel, M 2010, 'DIY media: A contextual background and some contemporary themes', in M Knobel and C Lankshear (eds), *DIY media: Creating, sharing and learning with new technologies*, Peter Lang, New York, NY, pp. 1–26.

Latour, B 2007, *Reassembling the social: An introduction to actor-network-theory*, Oxford University Press, Oxford.

Lingel, J and Naaman, M 2012, 'You should have been there, man: Live music, DIY content and online communities', *New Media & Society*, vol. 14, no. 2, pp. 332–349.

Mackay, H and Ivey, D 2004, *Modern media in the home: An ethnographic study*, John Libbey, Rome.

Malinowski, B 1922, *Argonauts of the Western Pacific: An account of native enterprise and adventure in the archipelagos of Melanesian New Guinea*, Routledge and Kegan Paul, London.

Mauss, M 1954, *The gift: The form and reason for exchange in archaic societies*, Psychology Press, London.

Meikle, G 2016, *Communication, sharing and visibility*, Routledge, London.

Miller, D and Tilley, C 1996, 'Editorial', *Journal of Material Culture*, vol. 1, no. 1, pp. 5–14.

Postill, J 2010, 'Introduction: Theorising media and practice', in B Bräuchler and J Postill, (eds), *Theorising media and practice*, Berghahn Books, Oxford and New York, NY, pp. 1–33.

Reckwitz, A 2002, 'Toward a theory of social practices: A development in culturalist theorizing', *European Journal of Social Theory*, vol. 5, no. 2, pp. 243–263.

Reckwitz, A 2012, 'Affective spaces: A praxeological outlook', *Rethinking History*, vol. 16, no. 2, pp. 241–258.

Schatzki, TR 1996, *Social practices: A Wittgensteinian approach to human activity and the social*, Cambridge University Press, Cambridge, MA.

Schatzki, TR 2001, 'Introduction: Practice theory', in TR Schatzki, K Knorr-Cetina and E von Savigny (eds), *The practice turn in contemporary theory*, Psychology Press, New York, NY, pp. 10–23.

Schatzki, TR 2002, *The site of the social: A philosophical account of the constitution of social life and change*, Pennsylvania State University Press, University Park, PA.

Shove, E, Pantzar, M and Watson, M 2012, *The dynamics of social practice: Everyday life and how it changes*, Sage, London.

Shove, E and Spurling, N (eds) 2013, *Sustainable practices: Social theory and climate change*, Routledge, London.

Silverstone, R 1994, *Television and everyday life*, Routledge, London.

Silverstone, R and Hirsch E 1992, *Consuming technologies: Media and information in domestic spaces*, Routledge, London.

Silverstone, R, Hirsch, E and Morley, D 1992, 'Information and communication technologies and the moral economy of the household', in R Silverstone, E Hisch and D Morley (eds), *Consuming technologies: Media and information in domestic spaces*, Routledge, London and New York, NY, pp. 15–31.

Skågeby, J 2008, *Gifting technologies: Ethnographic studies of end-users and social media sharing*, PhD thesis, Linköping University, Sweden.

Southerton, D, Olsen, W, Warde, A and Cheng, SL 2012, 'Practices and trajectories: A comparative analysis of reading in France, Norway, the Netherlands, the UK and the USA', *Journal of Consumer Culture*, vol. 12, no. 3, pp. 237–262.

Spaargaren, G, Weenink, D and Lamers, M (eds) 2016, *Practice theory and research: Exploring the dynamics of social life*, Routledge, London.

Taylor, C 1971, 'Interpretation and the sciences of man', *The Review of Metaphysics*, vol. 25, no. 1, pp. 3–51.

Taylor, C 2002, 'Modern social imaginaries', *Public Culture*, vol. 14, no. 1, pp. 91–124.

Van Dijck, J 2013, *The culture of connectivity: A critical history of social media*, Oxford University Press, Oxford and New York, NY.

Vannini, P 2009, 'Introduction', in P Vannini (ed), *Material culture and technology in everyday life*, Peter Lang Publishing, Inc., New York, NY.

Warde, A 2005, 'Consumption and theories of practice', *Journal of Consumer Culture*, vol. 5, no. 2, pp. 131–153.

Warde, A 2013, 'What sort of a practice is eating?', in E Shove and N Spurling (eds), *Sustainable practices: Social theory and climate change*, Routledge, London, pp. 52–78.

Wittel, A 2011, 'Qualities of sharing and their transformations in the digital age', *International Review of Information Ethics*, vol. 15, no. 9, pp. 3–8.

Section II

4   Boundaries of Disclosure

Introduction

This section of the book delves more deeply into my empirical data to describe how sharing is practised and to reveal detailed descriptions of the symbolic processes of sharing in digital culture and the complexities that arise in them.

This chapter considers the first of three significant themes to emerge in my data. I examine the boundaries of disclosures to demonstrate that sharing is an evolving social norm (van Dijck 2013). Boundaries are points of material, temporal and communicative difference. They may be actual or imagined, explicit or implicit. Participants work to negotiate multiple boundaries in their sharing practices, such as public/private and self/other. Disclosures, as acts of sharing secret or new information, are processes that hold potential to transcend, subvert or reinforce boundaries. This chapter examines how participants perceive and enact such boundaries in their sharing practices. By showing how sharing challenges perceptions of boundaries, I argue that, rather than being inherently familiar and frictionless, sharing is a social norm in a constant state of negotiation.

In discussing boundaries of disclosure, this chapter makes use of the data constructed in the participatory social maps produced during interviews. These are used to understand perceptions of boundaries and practices of enacting those boundaries. These social maps also prompt understanding and interpretations of abstract social relationality.

The chapter begins by identifying conceptualisations of boundaries in the relevant literature and proceeds to situate the topic of the chapter through the data. The remainder of the chapter is divided into three parts. The first part considers how participants perceive and enact boundaries in their social networks. Drawing on perceptions of privacy boundaries, the second part discusses how performances of sharing are motivated by privacy concerns for self and for others. Finally, this chapter addresses ways in which performances of sharing are shown to challenge the boundaries of disclosure, through processes of enculturation, competing desires and context collapse.

Boundaries of Privacy and Control

Disclosures are flows of informational data about, or pertaining to, one-self. Self-disclosure is the sharing of knowledge in the 'process of making the self known to others' (Jourard and Lasakow 1958, p. 91). There are three forms of self-disclosure: the peripheral or biographical (e.g. age); the intermediate by which the self may be known to others through attitudes, opinions and values; and core disclosures which include the private desires, needs, fears and beliefs of the individual (Altman and Taylor 1973). Intermediate and core disclosures are especially necessary for presentations of self in social encounters. In personal relationships, such disclosures build mutual trust and understanding (Laurenceau, Feldman-Barrett and Pietromonaco 1998; Rubin 1975). As discussed in Chapter 2, 'Theories of Sharing', boundaries of privacy and disclosure are a key focus in research on social media platforms (Wilson, Gosling and Graham 2012). Prior studies have noted that disclosures come with

> certain potential privacy risks, including unintentional disclosure of personal information, damaged reputation due to rumors and gossip, unwanted contact and harassment, vulnerability to stalkers or pedophiles, use of private data by a third party, hacking, and identity theft (boyd 2008; Debatin et al. 2009; Taraszow et al. 2008).
>
> (Wilson, Gosling and Graham 2012, p. 212)

Underpinning these research studies is a central concern with the boundaries of *privacy* and the control of those boundaries.

A suitable definition of privacy has long been problematic. Oft-cited lawyers Samuel Warren and Louis Brandeis (1890) define *privacy* as 'the right to be left alone'. Irwin Altman (1976) views privacy as interpersonal 'boundary-controlled processes'. For legal scholars such as Ruth Gavison (1980), a coherent concept of privacy is lacking. Privacy is often reduced to the notion of limited access:

> Our interest in privacy [. . .] is related to our concern over our accessibility to others: the extent to which we are known to others, the extent to which others have physical access to us, and the extent to which we are the subject of others' attention.
>
> (Gavison 1980, p. 423)

Such notions of privacy position desire for withdrawal in opposition to fear of surveillance, with the extreme being Hannah Arendt's (1958) 'radical privacy', where no one can see, hear, be seen or be heard. Privacy is also positioned as a series of tradeoffs, such as those that exist among the functionality of digital technologies (Agre and Rotenberg 1998), convenience (Culnan and Bies 2003; O'Neil 2001) and publicity (Tene 2011).

For example, Nicole Ellison et al. (2011) argue that individuals balance social benefits with privacy costs.

Sharing is often framed as a mandatory social process. Arendt (1958) identifies publicness as a necessary condition for the shared social world. We must both see and be seen (p. 52). Arendt describes sharing as integral to the human condition, for it inserts us into the public realm: 'This disclosure of "who" in contradistinction to "what" somebody is—his qualities, gifts, talents, and shortcomings, which he may display or hide—is implicit in everything somebody says and does' (Arendt 1958, p. 179). Disclosures are performed through speaking and what Arendt terms 'acting'. The public realm Arendt speaks of is not the public in the Habermasian sense, constructed through discourse; rather, it is the construction of a shared world with intimate others. Eva Illouz helps explain this distinction:

> the act of posting a profile allows the Internet [. . .] to convert the private self into a public performance. More exactly, the Internet makes the private self visible and publicly displayed to an abstract and anonymous audience, which, however, is not a public (in the Habermasian sense of that word) but rather an aggregation of private selves. On the Internet, the private psychological self becomes a public performance.
>
> (Illouz 2007, p. 78)

Jürgen Habermas (1989) describes public as the social environment in which ideas and thoughts can be exchanged, which emphasises discourse. Arendt highlights the performative aspects of self-presentation, which, in digital culture, manifest as public displays of disclosure that often fail to generate discourse or intimacy. Such disclosures are precarious, for they may be ignored, rejected or challenged by others.

Digital technologies provide a particular set of affordances for managing privacy as well as disrupting it. When sharing via digital technologies users must make overt decisions about their sharing actions: 'decisions of privacy, what to disclose and how, must be made a priori and explicitly' (Strater and Lipford 2008, p. 111). Furthermore, digital technologies present greater possibilities for context collapse, the 'sliding' together of multiple contexts or 'simultaneous co-presence' (Wittkower 2014). Dylan Wittkower's (2014) notion of context collapse is more nuanced and sophisticated than Michael Wesch's early description of the phenomenon as it occurs on YouTube, in which context collapse is

> an infinite number of contexts collapsing upon one another into that single moment of recording. The images, actions, and words captured by the [webcam] lens at any moment can be transported to anywhere on the planet and preserved (the performer must assume) for all time.
>
> (Wesch 2009, p. 23)

As Wittkower observes, Wesch does not meaningfully connect the contexts together, nor does he connect the user to the contexts of the content (Wittkower 2014). In actuality, context collapse is 'a more specific and threatening "sliding" wherein we know ourselves to be simultaneous present in different contexts each of which we identify with and have invested in' (Wittkower 2014). Wittkower draws attention to how processes of privacy are bounded together with presentations of self, as well as the way in which particular platforms and devices manifest context collapse differently. Sharing on YouTube poses a particular threat to presentations of self that are distinct to those of Facebook. Another factor of context collapse is the tenacity of digital content. In digital culture the persistence and permeability of social media content, and traces of technologically mediated interactions, mean audiences are always spatially and temporally precarious (boyd 2006).

Helen Nissenbaum (2009) argues that privacy in digital culture is managed through information flows, or 'contextual integrity', which she describes as disclosing information to the right people, in the right context. Contextual integrity involves a form of boundary work, which is the perceptual construction of divisions between aspects of one's social life. These divisions may be material, temporal or communicative. Explicitly identifying the labour inherent in such processes, Christena Nippert-Eng (2010) asks, 'What is the actual work involved in these processes, so critical to managing one's privacy?' (p. 2). Techniques of contextual integrity such as concealments and disclosures in the practice of maintaining access to oneself are selective and subjective. As well as the work of maintaining boundaries of self, work also occurs to maintain the boundaries of others.

While Nissenbaum (2009) describes privacy through information flows, a broader concept of privacy addresses multiple theories and justifications. Privacy law scholar Michael Birnhack argues,

> I list them in concentric circles, from the person outwards: individual psychological needs (autonomy and individuality; a space to develop one's identity and personhood; not to be gazed at; not to be de-contextualised against one's will), philosophical understanding of human beings (dignity); privacy as constitutive of intimate relationships, of professional relationships (attorney-client; physician-patient), and ultimately, as a social good, constituting a healthy and functioning community and the democratic state at large.
>
> (2011, p. 10)

Birnhack (2011) argues that privacy as control is a stronger conceptualisation, or meta-principle, than is contextual integrity, which is focused primarily on 'socio-technical systems that collect, process and transfer personal data' (p. 3). These do not account sufficiently for social norms, nor for organising units beyond context. Both contexts and norms are dynamic and 'unsettled' (p. 3). Privacy as control describes processes of autonomy over how one's personal information may be collected, processed and further used. The concept of control incorporates not only the withholding of information but also the needs of intimate and professional relationships, the philosophical and psychological needs, the functions of community and the nuances of the situated self embedded within evolving social norms (Birnhack 2011, p. 4; Cohen 2012).

The work that occurs at boundaries highlights the ways that privacy is determined by performed 'roles'. In any given scenario, a particular role (which exemplifies the standards of a particular group) is stressed over possible others. In order to convey a convincing performance, an individual may forgo, or claim to forgo, certain personal dimensions that are inconsistent with the present performance. A '"performance" may be defined as all the activity of a given participant on a given occasion which serves to influence in any way any of the other participants' (Goffman 1959, p. 15). Each role is performed as though it is the only one or, at least, the most important (Goffman 1959, p. 41):

> To be a given kind of person, then, is not merely to possess the required attributes, but also to sustain the standards of conduct and appearance that one's social grouping attaches thereto . . . A status, a position, a social place is not a material thing, to be possessed and then displayed; it is a pattern of appropriate conduct, coherent, embellished, and well articulated.
>
> (Goffman 1959, p. 75)

Sharing as an evolving social norm involves the negotiation of patterns of appropriate conduct. As the next section demonstrates, digital culture intensifies the negotiation of the boundaries of disclosures by confounding what Zeynep Tufekci (2008) describes as 'the boundary between the private and the public, the past and the future, disclosure and privacy' (p. 20).

Privacy in Practice

The following example from my data highlights the complexities of sharing as an evolving social norm.

Heather, a 27-year-old accountant working for a government organisation in Melbourne's central business district, was taking unusual action to keep a secret from her husband the day I interviewed her:

> My husband doesn't really read Facebook so it doesn't limit too much what I put on there, but obviously if it was something I didn't want him to know I wouldn't put it on Facebook. Like how I didn't put on there that I'm on holidays at the moment. That's what Twitter's for.
>
> (Heather)

Heather's husband was working away from home on a short-term con-
tract, and he was, according to her, miserable about this. Heather had
been pressured at work to take up some of her excess annual leave and
felt guilty that she was enjoying this time off without her husband's
knowledge. At the same time, she wanted to share that she was enjoying herself and make plans with other people to fill this free time. She
wasn't concerned that her husband would read Facebook himself but,
rather, that someone else in contact with her husband would read it
and comment to him about her additional leave. She planned to tell
him about her time off once he was back home. Between arranging and
taking the time off, Heather made tentative plans with a small group
of friends. She expressly told her friends her strategy for keeping her
husband in the dark until he returned to Melbourne and requested their
compliance in this act. She then monitored the communication with
these friends, which was potentially visible to her husband on social
media for breaches.

A number of friends were contacts on both Facebook and Twitter, so
Heather relied on them being selective about how they might disclose
her extra holiday days. She had to trust that they would confine their
responses to the social media platform she herself had selected. Heather
identifies that the mediation of this information is problematic in terms
of uncertain access. Heather effectively limits who she will share information with, and who might share her information, by selecting a specific interface based on her understanding of the affordances (perceived
features) of that interface and who is most likely to make use of those
affordances. In doing so she makes assumptions about how affordances
are acted upon. I discuss affordances in detail in Chapter 6.

Heather wanted to share her holiday activities because it vali-
dates the self she has constructed within particular circles on Twitter.
Heather carefully considered how she was presenting herself in this
selective sharing process. She wanted to avoid the label of 'bad wife'
and pointed to the reasons for her selectiveness as being determined
by her husband's needs. He was miserable being away from home, and
knowing she was on a trip would add to his disappointment about
working away from home and being unable to share her experiences.
She makes others complicit in her presentation of self. The amount
of work she undertakes to keep this information from her husband
highlights normative ideas about what information is shared between
husband and wife, ideas that are also laden with ideals and values of
the particular social context.

This description of Heather's performance of privacy in connection to
self builds on Erving Goffman's (1959) use of dramaturgical techniques
to explain how people engage in performances of self. The themes and
processes evident in this example are explored more substantially in the
remainder of this chapter.

Boundaries in Practice

Perceptions of Boundaries

As Heather's example earlier illustrates, participants have a sense of their personal boundaries of disclosure within their social networks, and these guide their sharing practices. The participatory social mapping method employed in this research makes material these perceptions of boundaries and prompts reflection on practices of enacting those boundaries. The social maps also prompt understanding and interpretations of social relationality and mediation.

Each of the participant's maps reproduced below show identification of 'cliques' which are 'socially perceived sub-groups' (Scott 2000) of interconnectivity from the perspective of the participant. These offer a different perspective to similar mapping methods such as sociograms, which identify attributes of networks (Hogan, Carrasco and Wellman 2007).

The social relationality between cliques differs between participants. Some participants produce egocentric maps (see Figure 4.1), which textually imply that there are no relational connections between cliques, though prompting during the drawing process reveals this not to be the case. Others make connections explicit in their mapping, signifying relational networks within cliques (see Figure 4.2) and across cliques (see Figure 4.3). Often, during the interview process, participants will iterate their social maps to show social relationality (see Figure 4.4), drawing

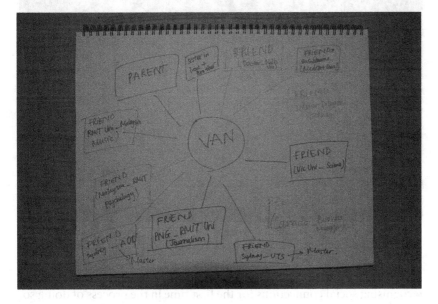

Figure 4.1 Donna's map, showing egocentric social mapping

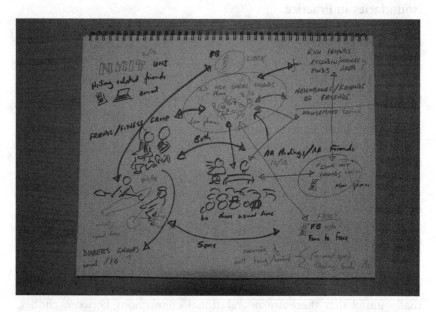

Figure 4.2 Jason's map, showing relational networks across cliques

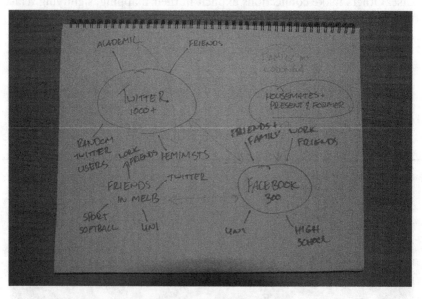

Figure 4.3 Addison's map, showing relational networks within cliques

additional lines between cliques as they identify connections, sometimes recognising social connections for the first time in the process of doing so. As one participant put it, 'I see a pattern forming. I love this mess, this is great' (Jason, 35-year-old writer).

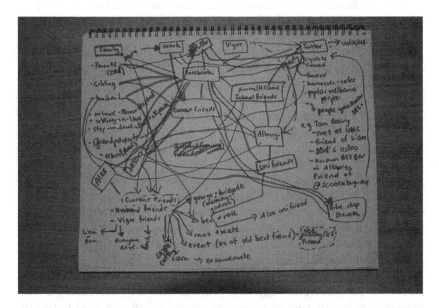

Figure 4.4 Heather's map, showing iterations of social relationality drawn during the interview process

Cliques are determined by multiple factors such as physical proximity, relationship types, perceptions of intimacy (which I argue is distinct to researcher-defined measures of tie strength) and how sharing practices are mediated. Excerpts from the interview transcripts show how these different relational factors are engaged within the mapping exercise, and how boundaries are contextualised and interrogated by participants in the process of their drawing:

> So, I'm drawing the groups of people that I'm connected with. You've got me in the middle and I have work associates, but within work I'll have managers and senior authority figures, I have co-workers which can border on being friends, I have clients, [of which] there are new, old and prospect . . . Outside of that I have things like social groups, so that would be gym, soccer and things. So, these will be friends, potential friends, acquaintances, strangers.
>
> (Shimmon, 28-year-old recruitment officer)

> The big one for me would be feminists. I find Twitter to be an awesome area to get support for that sort of stuff. That for me is a huge one. Can I put down random people, because there are just random Twitter users? So that's Twitter. I follow just over 1000 people. It's got to a stage whereby whenever I say something someone will reply to it. It takes a lot of maintenance.
>
> (Addison, 22-year-old PR manager)

Woah, there are connections, that's wild. That is freaky. For example, someone like Steve who I met on Twitter is linked in with [athletics club] but I didn't know that until I started. Then I have work and friends, but then I have people that I work with that I'm also friends with and do stuff outside work with, so they fit into both things, and they also fit into Facebook. But then get this! Dad who's on Facebook with me, his osteo is Tom who I met through [athletics club] and now I'm friends with him on Facebook. How do I picture that? I don't know how to do that.

(Hugo, 42-year-old IT specialist)

Participatory maps not only show perceptions of existing social connections but also acknowledge opportunities for new social connections. For example, Shimmon identifies potential clients in his work clique and potential friends in his social groups, as well as existing clients and friends. This is indicative of the dynamic nature of social groups.

Participatory social mapping identifies particular publics within cliques. Publics are 'the imagined community that emerges as a result of the intersection of people, technology, and practice' (boyd 2008). Addison recognises that her sharing practices are shaped by an imagined public of feminists, although her Twitter followers also include a significant proportion of other 'random' users. Addison also identifies that maintaining a presence through sharing requires ongoing labour, an important theme that I return to later.

Each of the excerpts quoted earlier illustrate how productive it is for participants to imagine distinctions between cliques in relation to the roles they perform in everyday life (Goffman 1959). Furthermore, the mapping exercise makes it apparent that the boundaries of disclosure do not correspond neatly onto social cliques; instead, boundaries are blurred by roles and by properties of mediation. In the following section, I investigate these boundary negotiations and their relationship with privacy.

Boundary Work

As discussed at the start of this chapter, privacy can be understood as a means of controlling and optimising access to self and others (Altman 1976; Birnhack 2011). Limiting access to particular content - such as information - is a common way of enabling privacy. Jose is a 23-year-old graphic designer who runs his own web design studio, which employs a number of subcontractors. Jose manages boundaries by controlling access to information about himself:

I don't talk about my work friends with my friends or vice versa. Even if I went out for dinner with my work friends and my friends asked me what I did the day beforehand I would say 'doing work'.

(Jose)

Jose's privacy is not motivated by secrecy but a desire to maintain contextual integrity between distinct roles. In this example of doing privacy, access to content is regulated according to interactions with others. This process is continually negotiated.

The boundaries of disclosure are layered and complicated. They are rarely absolute. For example, a 32-year-old software engineer living in Melbourne called Darryl describes how accessible he believes himself to be to his immediate family:

> I'm like an ochre. I have layers. With my family there are no layers, zero, at all. Layers are about how much thought, how considered I am with how I say things. The closer I get to people the less filter there becomes, I don't know if other people are like that? My parents and sister know exactly how I feel about pretty much anything.
>
> (Darryl)

Darryl feels he makes himself accessible to his family by speaking freely to them. Yet there are particular topics where this accessibility is, in fact, not present. Although Darryl feels close to his sister, he only disclosed details about his income to his parents when asking his family for advice on purchasing his first property:

> The only one who knows about my financial situation is my mum and dad. My sister doesn't know. Mum knows that I've started seeing someone but my sister doesn't because I haven't told her yet.
>
> (Darryl)

Even in the closest relationships, boundaries of disclosure exist. Some of these, such as Darryl's income, are based on preferences, while others are based on convenience and access. Darryl intends to tell his sister that he is dating but it feels rather dramatic to contact her with this explicit intention. Instead, he will wait for a more 'natural' opportunity to tell her.

Privacy is both dialectical and dynamic (Altman 1976; Birnhack 2011). For example, Heather withholds from sharing on Facebook so that she will have something to tell her father and close friend when she sees them:

> Sometimes I don't put things on Facebook because people like my dad or my friend Naomi see everything I do. Sometimes it's nice to tell them things that they don't know because otherwise they know everything, or they say things like 'oh yeah I saw that on Facebook'. Then you don't have anything to tell anybody.
>
> (Heather)

Heather keeps some information private from certain people so that she may share it with them at a specific moment and experience their reaction firsthand. Privacy is about selecting the moment of disclosure as well as selecting whether to disclose. While Heather freely shares information about herself on Facebook, she knows this is observed, or surveilled, by her father and her friend Naomi, among others. Doing privacy for her is not so much about avoiding surveillance as it is about selectively and dynamically optimising access to information about herself (Palen and Dourish 2003; Tufekci 2008). Furthermore, facilitating disclosure to particular individuals means keeping some information private from others. Retaining information to share face-to-face with her father and close friend means there are other people with whom she may not get to share the information with at all, such as those friends she rarely sees and maintains contact with primarily through Facebook.

Boundary work effects relative inaccessibility or accessibility. Boundary work is the 'process through which we organise potentially realm-specific matters, people, objects, and aspects of self' (Nippert-Eng 1996, p. 7). In other words, it affords control over access. For example, one way that Jose maintains boundaries between his professional and personal relationships is by curating two separate Facebook profiles:

> I use it [Facebook] professionally and personally. I've got two separate accounts. One is the business name and then one is my name. Clients see the professional account and I don't want clients to see my personal life. I sometimes don't want my friends to know what I'm doing at work. It's one of those things, I don't want my friends to write something indiscriminately on my work page.
>
> (Jose)

Jose extends this boundary work spatially:

> My work friends are usually just at work. My partner actually says 'why don't you invite them over?' and I'm like, 'no no, it's fine'. Work has to be separate from my closer relationships.
>
> (Jose)

Heather adopts similar boundary behaviour:

> The things I share online, especially on Twitter, is different to what other people know and what I want them to know. But it works the other way too, I mean there are things I won't put on Twitter or Facebook but I want to call my parents about.
>
> (Heather)

Heather gives consideration to what is accessible based on context, sharing only what she wishes with select audiences. She establishes boundaries around specific content or moments of disclosure.

Privacy is also a means of maintaining barriers to access. Using boundaries afforded by technologies can both help and hinder:

> There'[re] probably three or four people that I work with that I have on Facebook. Anybody else that I work with, even if I'm friends with them at work I probably won't add. People that I trust or am close to will comment on each other's Facebook. I don't mind if they bitch about work or I bitch about work. That's ok. But I wouldn't add anybody else that I work with especially if they were someone who worked under me. I would never ever add them.
>
> (Heather)

A further complication is that boundaries fluctuate. For example, Heather frequently adjusts access to her disclosures within specific interfaces:

> With my Twitter, I now have it unlocked but I used to have it that people had to request. I change my mind every now and then whether I want to or not. That's a sharing thing, because sometimes I'm quite happy to share anything, have everyone follow me and then I get a little bit freaked out and think hmmm, no! Just, the other day I unlocked it. I found it was annoying because it's harder to communicate with people when you put it on private.
>
> (Heather)

Her desire for privacy is in tension with her desire for public interaction. She must weigh her desire for communication against her perceptions of risk and vulnerability. Heather's perception of risk relates to her employer's policy for personal social media use rather than any anxieties about third-party data use, hacking or identity theft, which are often attributed to privacy concerns among users (Debatin et al. 2009; Taraszow et al. 2008).

According to Robert Wilson, Samuel Gosling and Lindsay Graham's (2012) review of literature on Facebook at the time of data collection, users are motivated by social benefits to share personal information despite there being privacy risks. Often the 'paradox' between privacy concerns and disclosures is due to the collapsing of core, intermediate and biographical data. While there is concern for the privacy of biographical data and metadata, this is in contrast with the propensity for personal disclosures of a core nature. More recent literature indicates people's privacy concerns have changed in the wake of the high profile events including the Cambridge Analytica scandal, fake news and Russian troll farms influencing users during the Brexit referendum and 2016 US election (Marwick and Hargittai 2018).

The notion of privacy as trade-off assumes oppositional motivations between privacy and the object of trade; however, privacy and sharing are separately motivated (Wilson, Gosling and Graham 2012, p. 212). Privacy is motivated by a risk of harm, while sharing is motivated by a desire for social intensity. The outcome of not sharing is a lack of social intensity, not exposure to harm. As well as being distinctly motivated, doing privacy and doing sharing are also distinct practices (Acquisti and Gross 2006; Stutzman and Kramer-Duffield 2010; Tufekci 2008).

The following examples show that privacy is an ongoing negotiation of multiple boundaries, indicating that not everything is for sharing. Navigating and controlling interface settings, relationships, roles, content and contexts is laborious boundary work. It also occurs in the deletion of content. For instance, Vanessa recalls a particular conversation on Facebook, which she later chose to delete:

> I woke up the next morning and thought hang on, was that completely public, or not public because my Facebook's locked? But the next morning I thought more or less anyone can read that. . . . It seemed very performative, a little bit too much so. Also it was an exchange between two people, not meant for anyone to see, even though there was nothing interesting about it at all.
>
> (Vanessa, 29-year-old university lecturer)

The conversation came about precisely because Vanessa had become reacquainted with an old friend through Facebook. The capacity to comment on another person's status update is long established. Indeed, in many ways status updates anticipate a response. In this case, a comment led to an extended conversation thread motivated by the duration of time since they had last been in contact. Reflecting back on this conversation the following morning, Vanessa identified a disjuncture between the accessibility which led to the conversation and the accessibility of the record of that conversation to other Facebook friends. She deleted the conversation thread to reestablish a more comfortable boundary for herself.

Strategies for privacy may be social or technical. Social strategies involve deciding what to share and with whom (Sleeper et al. 2013; Hogan 2010). Technical strategies involve manipulating platform or device features in order to define an audience for sharing. These may include changing privacy settings, creating lists out of network followers or friends, managing duplicate accounts and blocking or deleting members of a network (Debatin et al. 2009; Young and Quan-Haase 2009; Lampinen et al. 2011). While social and technical strategies of privacy involve the management of informational flows within or between networks, these are distinct to platform-oriented strategies that are intended to control access by a particular organisation to personal data. Both social and technical strategies are motivated by perceptions of immediate social consequences. Furthermore, technical and platform strategies are future-oriented, intended to block certain informational flows or limit audiences through a totality approach, meaning that a decision stands for multiple encounters.

Boundaries of interfaces can be at odds with perceptions of accessibility and privacy. For instance, even bounded audiences can feel public:

> The way the status feeds work [on Facebook] with people getting to see what other people are commenting on, it's all kind of lined up so that one conversation is viewable. Whereas Twitter is just a series of feeds, it's hard to follow and trace back a conversation on Twitter.
>
> (Darryl)

While Darryl's Twitter account is public, he carefully curates and limits his Facebook friends. Even so, he feels more comfortable expressing his personal opinions on Twitter because its publicness affords him a certain level of anonymity. A single tweet is quickly lost in a steady stream of content whereas on Facebook a status update remains on his profile page for a considerable time and is more readily searchable. Although Facebook is a bounded system, Darryl perceives it as more public. Here, publicness is not about quantifiable access but about feelings of risk and vulnerability.

Motivations for Maintaining Boundaries

So far, I have outlined strategies for doing privacy in relation to maintaining boundaries around self-disclosure. Motivations for such strategies relate to others, as well as to oneself.

As a social media user, Esel highlights the complex, subjective labour of sharing. There is a stark contradiction between Esel's statement quoted that follows, in which she identifies possible interpretations of her sharing practices, and the hyperbolic statements from social media platforms discussed in Chapter 1, in which sharing brings 'the world closer' and makes communication 'easy' (Chowdhury 2011). Considering what to share and what to keep private is, in part, a process of presenting and optimising access to self. People desire to share in ways that conform to their preferred presentations of self and, as such, they attempt to keep private what doesn't 'fit' with that performance:

> So I think like, I do 'like' this but do I like it enough to tell the whole world that I 'like' it because when people look at it they going to think 'oh she must love this brand' because she has 'liked' it on Facebook whereas I might not actually like it that much. Like, it's alright, I might have bought one top from there but I'm not in love with it.
>
> (Esel, 19-year-old university student)

Esel considers how the content she shares on Facebook shapes people's perception of her. While she doesn't feel the need to keep her appreciation of a particular brand of clothing secret, she doesn't wish to actively define herself by it and therefore elects to keep it private. I ask her about this relationship between self and sharing:

INTERVIEWER: Do you think what you share affects how people see you?
ESEL: Yes, of course! Because when you're sharing, you're saying something about yourself.

As Goffman's (1959) work shows, individuals are in a continual state of self-conceptualisation. Sharing is also a constitutive element of self-conceptualisation and sharing practices are part of the presentation of self. They convey information about the person and their relationship to others, which can be (mis)interpreted by others. Esel is selective about what she shares, primarily because she thinks others may view her negatively for it:

> I do have opinions about the world and politics and stuff but the fact is that I think a lot of people on my profile, a lot of my friends will judge me on it and say 'I can't be friends with you anymore, how could you have a stupid view'.
>
> (Esel)

Similarly, Donna likes to read articles on current political and social topics, but she doesn't feel comfortable posting this material to her Facebook profile because she thinks others won't find it interesting. She admits that 'there is a mindset that sharing certain things means you're cool' (Donna, 18-year-old university student). Sharing material that is funny is 'cool', whereas sharing material that communicates a serious political or social perspective is not. Similarly, a participant in *The New York Times*'s study discussed in Chapter 1, states, 'I try to share only information that will reinforce the image I'd like to present: thoughtful, reasoned, kind, interested and passionate about certain things' (The New York Times Customer Insight Group 2011). Choices are made regarding which tastes are to be performed and selectively shared. Presentations of self are constructed through selective performances of tastes crafted for particular audiences, through which the person is 'known' online (Ellison, Steinfield and Lampe 2006). This audience of peers is often perceived to be highly critical, making judgments and drawing meaning from every aspect of the profile, such as errors, timestamps, references to popular culture and other signifiers of taste (Ellison et al. 2006; Marwick and boyd 2011).

Selective sharing is a protective strategy that anticipates a critical audience. Consider these two quotes, which exemplify the desire to project a preferred presentation of self when sharing:

> What I share at work will typically be to ensure I protect my own brand within the business, so people see me as someone who is

professional and capable of doing their job especially to the likes of senior managers or people of authority . . . I don't share rumours or gossip at work. I think that undermines the individual and loses respect in a social group.

(Shimon)

You only share what you want people to know about you. I really hate it when people bitch on Facebook and say 'I hate my life' and that sort of thing because I'm like 'get a life'. . . . I would never share something on Facebook that made me look like a loser.

(Heather)

Shimon and Heather make decisions about their sharing based on how they wish to project themselves to others. In both responses, there is an awareness of social power based on what is concealed and revealed. For Shimon, revealing a propensity to gossip might undermine his integrity. While Heather wishes to appear popular and likeable, she is alert to incongruities and digressions that might imply she is not at the centre of a bustling social circle.

As mentioned earlier in this chapter, privacy strategies may be motivated by others' desires as well as our own. This may involve collaboratively managing others' boundaries of privacy and publicness or may involve adapting performances of sharing based on imagining how others may react. For example, Darryl is not concerned that others will think negatively of him if they are opposed to his political or religious views; rather, he is concerned he will offend them and cause upset: 'I don't want to be offensive in any way so I tend to censor a lot of what I put on Facebook' (Darryl). Similarly, Heidi considers what she shares so as not to hurt other people's feelings:

I share everything. There are probably things I don't share. I don't tell my closest friends how much they annoy me from time to time. I think that would be a bit of a dangerous thing to do. I mean there are things that I think and that I feel that are about the way *they* act. Sometimes I'd like to give them a piece of my mind [but] I just keep that to myself, so there are certainly things that I choose not to share with them.

(Heidi)

Heidi is aware that to tell her closest friends how much they annoy her at times would cause an upset in their relationship, so she keeps this information to herself. She feels that she willingly shares 'everything', with associated implications of openness and altruism, yet she also recognises potential conflicts, damage and consequences. In reality, this makes her unwilling to share 'everything'.

Selective sharing practices take into account what is presented about the self, how others might respond and what others hope for. For example,

Darryl refrains from disclosing certain topics of conversation because they are too intimate:

DARRYL: I never do anything intimate online.
INTERVIEWER: What's intimate?
DARRYL: Conversations about people and I guess how people think or react to certain things, what people's thoughts and opinions are to certain things, anything that's related to other people.

Darryl draws a distinction between what can be discussed online and what cannot be based on perceived consequences. Anything that relates to others and may have consequences for them, he considers too intimate to share. Airi Lampinen et al. (2011) argue that sharing - especially online sharing- 'is based on trust in others' collaboration in managing the boundaries of privacy and publicness—a shared norm of privacy boundary regulation online' (p. 4). For Darryl, people should have the right to decide for themselves what they wish to have shared about them (Acquisti and Gross 2006). Shimon describes a way of doing privacy that echoes Darryl's, rationalising, 'I would only share things if I'd been told that it's ok to share. I'm more than capable of listening to things that are of a personal nature and keeping it to myself' (Shimon). In conjunction with his desire to be considered trustworthy, Shimon is also aware that as a secret keeper, privacy is a collaborative process. Shimon works to maintain others' presentations of self by keeping their secrets private. As Alice Marwick and danah boyd (2011) explain, '[i]ndividuals work together to uphold preferred self-images of themselves and their conversation partners, through strategies like maintaining (or "saving") face, collectively encouraging social norms, or negotiating power differentials and disagreements' (p. 123).

Participants monitor responses to their own presentations as a secondary shaping influence and attempt to limit what others may share on their behalf. Privacy settings and filters to accommodate or limit sharing are constantly in flux, as terms of service are updated, new contacts added and redundant ones removed or as personal preferences change. Practices of sharing also shift in response to moments of crisis. For instance, James filters and approves photos in which he is tagged before they appear on his profile page because he is conscious that he might be represented in other people's photos in a way that is different to what he prefers. He does this to attempt to control any presentations of self that might contradict the presentation he has crafted himself rather than trusting others. Tagging was a feature of Facebook at the time of the interview, where users labelled photographs with profile names, associating that photo with the profile owner. Profiles can include a collection of personal photographs as well as photographs taken by other people that have been labelled or tagged. Profile owners can select whether to have photos taken by others and tagged automatically displayed on their profile or suspended until approved. When I interviewed Vanessa, a university lecturer, she had only recently started to filter photos. This followed an incident in which she was tagged by a friend in some personal photos, which Vanessa would have preferred remain private. The photos created an uncomfortable situation for Vanessa, due to their provocative nature:

> There was a case a few weeks ago when someone tagged some photos of me from a few years ago at a nightclub . . . I was so angry I deleted the tags straight away and sent a private message saying I have people from work on Facebook. I was a little bit worried about who had seen it by the time I took the tag off because I think there was about an hour between. It turned out not many people had but it was a very fraught moment for me.
>
> (Vanessa)

At the time of the incident, Vanessa had her Facebook profile set to automatically display any photos in which she was tagged. The incident showed that, in opposition to what Marwick and boyd (2011) argue, she could not rely on others to be complicit with her desired presentation of self. This prompted her to adjust her privacy settings to prevent others from sharing photos on her timeline.

Challenges to Boundaries

Sliding Contexts

Context collapse is a threat to privacy, as experienced by interview participant Vanessa when photos of her younger self in a nightclub were shared on Facebook, making them visible to her work colleagues and supervisors without her permission. Context collapse occurs when what was inaccessible suddenly becomes accessible. To give another example, when Michelle began dating a colleague, she didn't want her elder brother to know because her new date was also a mutual colleague. To avoid her brother finding out, she kept the relationship secret from other colleagues, her family and many of her friends:

> One night my brother called me and said 'can you come and get me from the station, I've just been attacked'. He was pretty shaken up. The next night I was due to go and have dinner with Aaron and I thought 'well, I'm not going to leave him [my brother] here by himself so I'm just going to tell him' so I told my brother what was going on and took him to dinner. So it was Aaron, my brother and I for dinner which was interesting.
>
> (Michelle)

Although telling her brother about her relationship resulted in an uncomfortable dinner for the three of them, it was preferable to leaving her brother alone. Boundaries are constantly in flux and must be renegotiated as contexts shift and new ones emerge.

The proliferation of content on social media platforms deepens and widens a range of potential contexts, which also amplifies threats to privacy. A single image or post on Facebook may not convey a great deal, but when combined with data stratified across months, years and several platforms, privacy becomes cumulatively challenged. The proliferation of content provides the opportunity for practices such as 'Facebook stalking', which, although transgressive, is not always intentional:

> I've been guilty of that. I'll see something funny and I'll click on [a person's] page to see if they've posted anything else and then I'll get distracted because they posted a picture, so I'll look at the picture then I'll look at other pictures. If someone walks into the room at that moment it'll just be really awkward because you don't—when you first thought of going on Facebook—say I'm going to look at their profile pictures. It's just a little bit creepy. But you wind up there anyway. People will deny they Facebook stalk because they don't do it intentionally, but they do it, without knowing that they are doing it. I reckon everyone does it.
>
> (Donna)

> On people's Facebook walls you can scroll down and look at every single one of their Facebook posts and photos they put up . . . that's why I don't post much on my wall in the first place because you don't want someone you don't know that well to be sifting through all of your Facebook information. You think it's a little bit harmless and it sort of is but at the same time, is it really their business? But then it is a public space, Facebook.
>
> (James, 18-year-old university student)

At the time of my data collection, people spoke of 'going on' Facebook, where their main privacy concern was 'Facebook stalking'. James demonstrates a fluctuation between positions of ease and unease. Both Donna and James acknowledge that it is probable that many will have participated in Facebook stalking at some stage, they also identify that it is a practice few will admit to engaging in. In fact, there is a tendency to deny such behaviour is possible. As Donna illustrates, in a further comment, 'why is it people put the information up but get freaked out when people go and look at it?' (Donna).

While context collapse can indeed cause tensions, it is important to note that participants do have strategies to mitigate such risks (Lampinen et al. 2011). Such strategies include manipulation of privacy controls, selecting channels of communication based on privacy, limiting access to content and self-censorship.

Learning Norms

Privacy and sharing practices differ because the latter are socially learned (Burke, Marlow and Lento 2010; Merten 1999). Indeed, Moira Burke, Cameron Marlow and Thomas Lento (2010) established that new Facebook users modified their sharing practices based on the performances modelled by their peers. In addition, the authors found that performances modelled in the first two weeks of Facebook use shaped new users' future sharing practices (Burke, Marlow and Lento 2010), highlighting processes of enculturation for sharing.

Boundaries of privacy also require social learning and, potentially, intervention:

> A couple of times I've got in trouble because of stuff I discussed with my family about [my girlfriend]. One of those things was to do with our sexual life. I discussed it with my parents because for me it doesn't matter, but I guess it's not socially acceptable for them to know what's happening in our personal relationship. She explained to me many times before I actually got that I couldn't discuss it with my family.
>
> (Jose)

Until his girlfriend intervened, Jose regularly - and some might say nightmarishly - discussed his sex life with his family, including his parents. Growing up in a tightly knit family, Jose had always felt able to share everything and anything, without having to consider whether it was, in fact, appropriate. As his relationship with his girlfriend developed, Jose discovered that his boundaries of privacy needed to be moderated according to his partner's boundaries. Furthermore, adapting his sharing practices gave him greater awareness that there were, in fact, boundaries of social acceptability, which he had regularly overstepped:

> The next time I talked to somebody about something sexual, their facial expression changed. I didn't see that before, but after she talked to me, I saw that they weren't happy to know about that sort of stuff. I saw that they didn't really want to know about it, and my partner didn't want to tell them. I thought 'well this is something that must be true, she must be right. It must be something I can't share with everybody'.
>
> (Jose)

Jose discovered there were limits to what could be openly shared with close family and acquaintances. Through his girlfriend's intervention he acquired a new understanding of what was private and learnt to recognise social signals that indicated he was crossing such boundaries, or 'oversharing'.

In practising sharing, subjects bring themselves into a sense of belonging with others. Lauren Berlant (2008) uses the term 'communitas' to describe the affective intensity of this belonging. For Berlant, the affective intensity of belonging comes through the feeling that others feel the same way. If the experience of sharing brings people into a sense of affective belonging with others, then oversharing can also bring about a sense of belonging. Oversharing can be seen as a particularly affective form of longing that both acknowledges normative boundaries of personal disclosure while also resisting or moving beyond them in search of greater intimacy.

Sharing practices, even within the boundaries of existing social norms, can be fraught with anxiety. As Miller (2002) argues, anxiety 'always threatens the enterprise of going public with private stories' (p. 137). This is implied in Michelle's remark: 'You don't want to do any oversharing on Facebook' (Michelle). Not everyone is understanding about oversharing, whether online or in person. More often, moments of oversharing are met with fierce backlash:

> In one of my classes this girl said 'I couldn't believe it when one of my friends got her mum to help put her tampon in' or something, and all these other girls were like 'oh my God, oversharing! No one wants to know about that'. People don't want to know about that sort of stuff.
>
> (Esel)

Often oversharing is framed as a lack of compartmentalisation, with consequences for emotional or social wellbeing. Indicative of the way oversharing has emerged as a contemporary social dilemma, when Intel conducted their 'State of Mobile Etiquette Survey' on perceptions and trends in mobile etiquette, many of the mobile manners reported as problematic related specifically to oversharing (Intel 2012a). Oversharing was considered to be volunteering too many details, especially banal details, or gripes about one's life. Those surveyed thought that people share too much information about themselves online, with over 85% of Australian respondents believing people should be more considered about what they share online, including the ways that it may affect how others perceive them (Intel 2012c).

Oversharing can also be framed as sharing information that is inappropriately accessed. For example, Sherry Turkle argues that 'people pay a psychological price for seeing information about former friends and spouses and colleagues that they really shouldn't be seeing' (cited in Paul 2012). It's not good for our emotional health, she argues, as 'it makes people feel bad because they know they shouldn't look at this stuff—but they can't help it!' (Turkle cited in Paul 2012). Further demonstrating this practice, the Intel survey stated that '[o]ver a quarter of teens in Australia (26%) report they have kept up with the lives of ex-girlfriends or ex-boyfriends with information they find online' (Intel 2012c). Yet the survey also identified the centrality of sharing to relationships. Sharing enables people to feel connected to one another, and sharing information online is often used to stay up to date with loved ones. Furthermore, practices of sharing intensify the social bonds between those involved. Sharing is a means of fostering and strengthening relationships. It does this by pushing beyond existing boundaries of social norms, extending them into new intensities or directions. I argue that the risk of over-reaching, or oversharing, is inherently present in these processes of social intensification. Furthermore, my research reveals that oversharing is actually a productive social process as it serves to assert and establish new social norms.

Genevieve Bell makes a similar assertion:

> As new technologies, devices and services appear, everyone will continue to sort out how all of this will fit into our lives—and how we use these devices and services to connect with others. It has become so much easier to share the small details of our lives with our friends and family, but I think some people are still figuring out the right balance between staying connected and 'over-sharing'.
>
> (cited in Intel 2012b)

In contemporary digital culture, there is a constant negotiation about what it means to be a digital subject. Oversharing is a part of this negotiation. The notion of oversharing as content being made public when it ought to have remained private is limited and neglects the complex social relations and desires being enacted in the process.

Reprieve and Assistance

Sharing is a way of enacting social relations and of forming social bonds. In illustration of this, one of my participants, Maya, a 46-year-old public administrator, shares her personal feelings about her workplace with a few select colleagues on Facebook Messenger. In doing so, they identify each other as being part of a supportive circle of close contacts and distinguish themselves from the other colleagues whom they find problematic:

> A lot of it has to do with work . . . just having a whinge about what's gone wrong. There are some very strong characters that we have to cope with at work so it's good to go out and get it off your chest.
>
> (Maya)

The secrecy of a private conversation thread, unbeknown to colleagues, elaborates on meanings of sharing and intensifies the social connection between the people involved. Sharing secrets is a way of signifying emotional bonds between people, as Vaughan (1990) and Nippert-Eng (2010) have shown in their respective work on practices of conceal-ment. Sharing as an intentional process of social intensification reoccurs throughout my data. The previous example highlights that sharing prac-tices make perceived social boundaries, between those in the conversa-tion thread and those who are not, visible.

Conclusion

Through an examination of the boundaries of disclosure, this chapter has argued that sharing is an evolving social norm involving negotiations around privacy. Boundaries are necessary because of privacy concerns and power hierarchies in relationships and participatory social maps show how people perceive boundaries in their social networks. The dis-cussions that follow demonstrate the labours of enacting these boundar-ies with specific attention to privacy. This chapter has argued that sharing requires careful negotiation of desires for, and challenges to, privacy, both for oneself and for others. Contexts for sharing are unsettled and dynamic. Finally, identifying particular challenges to the boundaries of disclosure illustrates how sharing as a social norm is always in the pro-cess of being negotiated.

As the data discussed in this chapter show, sharing can provoke anxi-eties around norms and reciprocity. Digital subjects negotiate not only social norms but also platform affordances. Through their descriptions of sharing practices, the participants in my study make it clear they are very aware of the labours involved in negotiating social norms and platform conventions. They also demonstrate that the process of negotiating norms sometimes involves purposeful contravention in response to a longing for affective intensity. Oversharing can be viewed as a decisive form of 'refusal of the terms of the conventional world' (Berlant 2008, p. 268). Oversharing is therefore more than just 'wanting to shout out loud about one's uniqueness' (Agger 2012, p. 4). It is a practice that purposefully and consciously pushes past socially inscribed limits in search of mutuality and intimacy. As Berlant argues, 'an intimate public is an achievement' borne through affective labour (Berlant 2008, p. viii). Applying Berlant's concept of the intimate public to oversharing, and to sharing practices more broadly, allows us to understand how oversharing plays a role in a search of community.

Contexts for sharing are dynamic and unsettled, especially in ephemeral digital contexts where social media platform affordances (e.g., privacy settings) can shift with little notice. Platforms seek out every opportunity to encourage users to provide more data about themselves. It is therefore highly likely that boundaries of appropriate sharing, whatever they might mean in any given context, will also shift over time. During these shifts, people will be most vulnerable to oversharing.

It is also highly likely that people will purposefully overshare as a means of exploring (and exposing) the dynamic nature of platform affordances and social norms. The data presented in this chapter indicate an acute awareness of boundaries of sharing among social media users and suggest oversharing is an active and purposeful practice. Aware of the tension between the social media platforms' desires for personal data and their own desires for belonging, digital subjects navigate norms of sharing through privacy, platform affordances and social expectations. Oversharing is a part of this process, as norms of sharing are negotiated by platforms and users alike.

Drawing on Berlant's concept of 'communitas' (2008) and empirical data on sharing practices by digital subjects, I have demonstrated how reciprocity is central for bringing participants into affective intensity with others. New norms are legitimated through reciprocity. Digital subjects engage in oversharing in a process of making themselves vulnerable in anticipation of reciprocity. Oversharing is thus a productive social process as it asserts and establishes new social norms. This reframing of oversharing highlights how limits of social norms are tested and enacted in digital contexts as an ongoing process.

Returning to the scenario that opened this chapter, Heather's wanting to keep her extra leave secret from her husband, in the interview I raised the question, '[W]hy share on a social media platform something that needed to be kept a secret?' Heather's reason was that she wanted to share the experience those extra days off afforded her with others, even though she didn't want specific people to know—mainly her husband and those who might tell her husband. This raises a number of interesting ideas around the boundaries, immediacy, causality and reciprocity of sharing. The experience had to be shared *as it was occurring* rather than a week or so later so that others could respond and validate her experience. Heather shares her activities on Twitter out of a desire for response and validation, which is itself a significant aspect of sharing practice. As is discussed in the following chapter, Heather's experience highlights the centrality of reciprocity.

References

Acquisti, A and Gross, R 2006, 'Imagined communities: Awareness, information sharing and privacy on the Facebook', *Proceedings of privacy enhancing technologies workshop*, Springer, Cambridge, pp. 36–58.

Agre, PE and Rotenberg, M (eds) 1998, *Technology and privacy: The new landscape*, MIT Press, Boston, MA.

Altman, I 1976, 'Privacy: A conceptual analysis', *Environment and Behavior*, vol. 8, no. 1, pp. 7–29.

Altman, I and Taylor, DA 1973, *Social penetration: The development of interpersonal relationships*, Holt, Rinehart & Winston, New York, NY.

Arendt, H 1958, *The human condition*, University of Chicago Press, Chicago, IL.

Berlant, L 2008, *The female complaint: The unfinished business of sentimentality in American culture*, Duke University Press, Durham, NC and London.

Birnhack, M 2011, 'A quest for a theory of privacy: Context and control', *Jurimetrics*, vol. 51, no. 4.

boyd, d 2006, 'Friends, Friendsters, and MySpace top 8: Writing community into being on social network sites', *First Monday*, vol. 11, no. 12.

boyd, d 2008, *Taken out of context: American teen sociality in networked publics*, PhD thesis, University of California Berkeley.

Burke, M, Marlow, C and Lento, T 2010, 'Social network activity and social well-being', *Postgraduate Medical Journal*, vol. 85, pp. 455–459.

Chowdhury, A 2011, 'Global pulse', *Twitter weblog*, viewed 13 September 2012, <http://blog.twitter.com/2011/06/global-pulse.html>.

Cohen, J 2012, *Configuring the networked self: Law, code, and the play of everyday practice*, Yale University Press, New Haven, CT.

Culnan, MJ and Bies, RJ 2003, 'Consumer privacy: Balancing economic and justice considerations', *Journal of Social Issues*, vol. 59, no. 2, pp. 323–343.

Debatin, B, Lovejoy, JP, Horn, A and Hughes, BN 2009, 'Facebook and online privacy: Attitudes, behaviors, and unintended consequences', *Journal of Computer-Mediated Communication*, vol. 15, no. 1, pp. 83–108.

Ellison, N, Steinfield, C and Lampe, C 2006, 'Spatially bounded online social networks and social capital: The role of Facebook', *Proceedings of the Annual Conference of the International Communication Association*, vol. 36, pp. 1–37.

Ellison, N, Steinfield, C and Lampe, C 2011, 'Connection strategies: Social capital implications of Facebook-enabled communication practices', *New Media & Society*, vol. 13, pp. 873-892.

Gavison, R 1980, 'Privacy and the limits of law', *Yale Law Journal*, vol. 89, no. 3, pp. 421–471.

Goffman, E 1959, *The presentation of self in everyday life*, Anchor Books, New York, NY.

Habermas, J 1989, *The structural transformation of the public sphere: An inquiry into a category of Bourgeois society*, trans. T Burger with F Lawrence, MIT Press, Cambridge, MA.

Hogan, B 2010, 'The presentation of self in the age of social media: Distinguishing performances and exhibitions online', *Bulletin of Science, Technology & Society*, vol. 30, no. 6, pp. 377–386.

Hogan, B, Carrasco, J and Wellman, B 2007, 'Visualizing personal networks: Working with participant aided sociograms', *Field Methods*, vol. 19, pp. 116–144.

Illouz, E 2007, *Cold intimacies: The making of emotional capitalism*, Polity, Cambridge.

Intel 2012a, '2012 State of mobile etiquette and digital sharing: Intel survey', *Intel Corporation*, viewed 8 March 2019, <http://download.intel.com/newsroom/kits/mobileetiquette/pdfs/Mobile_Etiquette_2012_FactSheet.pdf.

Intel 2012b, 'Intel survey finds digital over sharing is leading to mobile etiquette Faux Pas', *Intel Corporation*, viewed 9 March 2019, <http://newsroom.intel.com/community/intel_newsroom/blog/2012/05/08/intel-survey-finds-digital-over-sharing-is-leading-mobile-etiquette-faux-pas)>.

Intel 2012c, 'Intel annual mobile etiquette study examines online sharing behaviours around the world', *Intel Corporation*, viewed 8 March 2019, <http://newsroom.intel.com/community/intel_newsroom/blog/2012/09/05/intel-annual-mobile-

etiquette-study-examines-online-sharing-behaviors-around-the-world-global-perception-of-oversharing-revealed>.

Jourard, SM and Lasakow, P 1958, 'Some factors in self disclosure', *Journal of Abnormal and Social Psychology*, vol. 56, pp. 91–98.

Lampinen, A, Lehtinen, V, Lehmuskallio, A and Tamminen, S 2011, 'We're in it together: Interpersonal management of disclosure in social network services', *Proceedings of the SIGCHI conference on human factors in computing systems*, ACM, pp. 3217–3226.

Laurenceau, JP, Feldman-Barrett, L and Pietromonaco, PR 1998, 'Intimacy as an interpersonal process: The importance of self-disclosure, partner disclosure, and perceived partner responsiveness in interpersonal exchanges', *Journal of Personality and Social Psychology*, vol. 74, pp. 1238–1251.

Marwick, AE and boyd, d 2011, 'I tweet honestly, I tweet passionately: Twitter users, context collapse, and the imagined audience', *New Media & Society*, vol. 13, no. 1, pp. 114–133.

Marwick, AE and Hargittai, E 2018, 'Nothing to hide, nothing to lose? Incentives and disincentives to sharing information with institutions online', *Information, Communication & Society*, published online 29 March 2018, DOI: 10.1080/1369118X.2018.1450432.

Merten, DE 1999, 'Enculturation into secrecy among junior high school girls', *Journal of Contemporary Ethnography*, vol. 28, no. 2, pp. 107–137.

Miller, N 2002, *But enough about me: Why we read other people's lives*, Columbia University Press, New York, NY and Chichester.

The New York Times Customer Insight Group 2011, *The psychology of sharing*, viewed 5 September 2012, <http://nytmarketing.whsites.net/mediakit/pos/>.

Nippert-Eng, C 1996, 'Calendars and keys: The classification of "home" and "work"', *Sociological Forum*, vol. 11, no. 3, pp. 563-582.

Nippert-Eng, C 2010, *Islands of privacy*, University of Chicago Press, Chicago, IL.

Nissenbaum, H 2009, *Privacy in context: Technology, policy, and the integrity of social life*, Stanford University Press, Palo Alto, CA.

O'Neil, D 2001, 'Analysis of internet users' level of online privacy concerns', *Social Science Computer Review*, vol. 19, no. 1, pp. 17–31.

Palen, L and Dourish, P 2003, 'Unpacking privacy for a networked world', *Proceedings of the SIGCHI conference on human factors in computing systems*, ACM, pp. 129–136.

Paul P 2012, 'Don't tell me, I don't want to know', *The New York Times*, viewed 9 March 2019, www.nytimes.com/2012/02/12/fashion/tmi-i-dont-want-to-know.html.

Rubin, Z 1975, 'Disclosing oneself to a stranger: Reciprocity and its limits', *Journal of Experimental Social Psychology*, vol. 11, no. 3, pp. 233–260.

Scott, J 2000, *Social network analysis: A handbook*, Sage, London.

Sleeper, M, Balebako, R, Das, S, McConahy, AL, Wiese, J and Cranor, LF 2013, 'The post that wasn't: Exploring self-censorship on Facebook', *Proceedings of the 2013 conference on Computer supported cooperative work*, ACM, pp. 793–802.

Strater, K and Lipford, HR 2008, 'Strategies and struggles with privacy in an online social networking community', *Proceedings of the 22nd British HCI group annual conference on people and computers: Culture, creativity, interaction*, Liverpool John Moores University, Liverpool, pp. 111–119.

Stutzman, F and Kramer-Duffield, J 2010, 'Friends only: Examining a privacy-enhancing behavior in Facebook', *Proceedings of the 28th International Conference on Human Factors in Computing Systems*, CHI 2010, Atlanta, Georgia, USA, April 10–15, pp. 1553-1562.

Taraszow, T, Arsoy, A, Shitta, G and Laoris, Y 2008, 'How much personal and sensitive information do cypriot teenagers reveal in Facebook?', *Proceedings from 7th European conference on e-learning*, ACI, Reading, pp. 871–876.

Tene, O 2011, 'Privacy: The new generations', *International Data Privacy Law*, vol. 1, no. 1, pp. 15–27.

Tufekci, Z 2008, 'Can you see me now? Audience and disclosure regulation in online social network sites', *Bulletin of Science, Technology & Society*, vol. 28, no. 1, pp. 20–36.

Van Dijck, J 2013, *The culture of connectivity: A critical history of social media*, Oxford University Press, Oxford and New York, NY.

Vaughan, D 1990, *Uncoupling: Turning points in intimate relationships*. Random House, London.

Warren, SD and Brandeis, LD 1890, 'Right to privacy', *Harvard Law Review*, vol. 4, pp. 193–220.

Wesch, M 2009, 'YouTube and you: Experiences of self-awareness in the context collapse of the recording webcam', *Explorations in Media Ecology*, vol. 8, no. 2, pp. 19–34.

Wilson, RE, Gosling, SD and Graham, LT 2012, 'A review of Facebook research in the social sciences', *Perspectives on Psychological Science*, vol. 7, no. 3, pp. 203–220.

Wittkower, DE 2014, 'Facebook and dramauthentic identity: A post-Goffmanian theory of identity performance on SNS', *First Monday*, vol. 19, no. 4.

Young, AL and Quan-Haase, A 2009, 'Information revelation and internet privacy concerns on social network sites: A case study of Facebook', *Proceedings of the fourth international conference on communities and technologies*, ACM, pp. 265–274.

5 Reciprocity and Other Labours

Introduction

In the previous chapter I discussed boundaries of self, others, privacy and control in sharing. The audience, as actual and imagined other, has haunted these discussions. In this chapter I focus on the expectations and conditions of reciprocity in sharing, especially in regard to the role of the other. Examining reciprocity strategies provides further insight into imaginaries and serves to highlight some of the labours of sharing.

This chapter considers reciprocity as a 'condition of possibility' for sharing (Kennedy and Milne 2013). Sharing is a process that holds expectations of reciprocity. I begin by exploring these expectations as they are framed in the existing literature. The second section examines how reciprocity is constituted and implicitly enacted in sharing practices. This leads into a discussion of how expectations are bound up with performances of reciprocity. Finally, the chapter details how the necessities of negotiation with an imagined complicate reciprocal practices.

Reciprocity

In Chapter 1, I outlined how reciprocity implies a mutual or cooperative exchange. Reciprocity functions to extend the boundaries of communities by bringing others into the exchange. Reciprocity is shown to be a key factor in the communication process, although one that is often overlooked (Solove 2007; Tufekci 2008). Bart Cammaerts (2011) declares that 'all forms of digital sharing involves degrees of reciprocity' (p. 47). Acknowledging the centrality of reciprocity in the communication process attends to complexity which operates beyond the person sharing (to whom most attention is usually paid).

I return to Erving Goffman's (1959) dramaturgical metaphor, in which the audience has a responsibility to participate in performances. Performers segregate audiences so as not to confuse the roles they are expected to play. An individual performs a particular role on the presumption that this audience will not be present when they perform another role, in another setting. The audience cooperates with the performer to foster this impression through reciprocal influence. An interaction 'may be roughly defined as the *reciprocal* influence of individuals upon one another's actions when in one another's immediate physical presence' (Goffman 1959 p. 15, emphasis mine).

While Goffman argues that audiences have a responsibility to reciprocate the performance, Kate Crawford (2009) argues for a responsibility to listen, particularly in context of social network sites. Crawford (2009) positions listening as a form of reciprocity. She defines reciprocal listening in Twitter not only as 'hearing and responding to comments and direct messages' (p. 530) but also as what she calls background listening: 'the disclosures made in social media spaces develop a relationship with an audience of listeners. Further, those background listeners are necessary to provoke disclosures of any kind' (Crawford 2009, pp. 528–529). The *possibility* of reciprocity is an enabling condition for disclosure.

Listening acknowledges the centrality of the other, whose active stance has been elided by the deployment of the term *lurker*, a person who spends time online observing interactions without participating. Such pejorative labels omit the necessity of the reciprocal (although silent) other. Crawford views listening as a necessary participatory act; I also argue that listening is participatory and reciprocal in that engagement with the text or utterance renders it 'heard'. While listeners or lurkers do not contribute in the same manner as more visible or vocal participators, they play a contributing role. Listening is therefore a receptive, reciprocal practice of dynamic attentiveness (Crawford 2009, p. 527).

The material conditions of listening frame the dyadic of sharing within an ideology of social connectivity. What makes listening so powerful as a metaphor is its interdependency and dynamic relation to speaking (Bickford 1996, p. 145). Nick Couldry (2009) argues,

> The reason we need to listen—and the reason why, arguably, depending on how we want to frame things, we have an 'obligation' to listen—is that all human beings have the capacity for voice, to give an account of their lives
>
> (p. 580)

Reciprocity constructs social reality as an experience of the world shaped through a shared existence with others (Arendt 1958, p. 52). In Aristotelian thinking, reciprocal sharing is the binding force of all friendships (Vallor 2012, p. 189). Adopting a philosophical approach, Dylan Wittkower (2013, p. 2) argues that reciprocity in social media platforms is an intermediate mode of being-with, where sharing creates the possibility of presence and asynchronous shared experience. Drawing from Heidegger's (1962) mode of sociability, Wittkower argues that sharing brings about an alteration in our being-with others. Sharing allows people to 'experience an object of attention together asynchronously and at a distance' (2013, p. 1) through the reciprocal act which retroactively constructs the shared experience. The sharer constructs the possibility of presence, offering an object with the future possible ideal of being shared. In all regards, sharing needs to be received, and receipt acknowledged, for being-with to be constituted. Such retroactive constructions of shared experience can be disruptive and unwelcome.

Transgressive sharing takes several forms. The sharer may construct an ideal of themselves that does not fit with the receiver's ideal. The sharer may not reach the intended receiver or may over-reach to a wider audience than intended, that is, through context collapse. This presents another potential for transgression, as the unintended receiver may, through reciprocation, be retroactively co-present in an experience unintended by the sharer. Reciprocity is a significant factor in social media platform–related anxieties, where the anticipation of reciprocation or the abundance of reciprocation through context collapse can cause distress as in oversharing.

Reciprocity can be understood as a 'pattern of exchange through which the mutual dependence of people, brought about by the division of labour, is realised' (Gouldner 1960, pp. 169–170). It is important to differentiate between the immaterial labour of content production and circulation, as discussed in Chapter 1, and the affective labour that is also evident in these narratives and to which Gouldner (1960) refers. As Michael Hardt and Antonio Negri describe,

> [t]he other face of immaterial labor is the affective labor of human contact and interaction [. . .] This labor is immaterial, even if it is corporeal and affective, in the sense that its products are intangible, a feeling of ease, well-being, satisfaction, excitement or passion.
>
> (2000, pp. 290–292)

Although Hardt and Negri identify affective labour as a 'type of immaterial labor' that 'involves the production and manipulation of affect and requires (virtual or actual) human contact, labor in the bodily mode' (Hardt and Negri 2000, p. 293), they do little to elaborate on the concept of affect. The 'affective turn' in the humanities and social sciences is advanced through a focus on emotions and the body, drawing on queer and feminist theory, respectively, and a correspondence between 'the power to act and the power to be affected' (Hardt 2007, p. x). To paraphrase Michael Hardt, the term *affective labour* draws together the (gendered) emotional, care-oriented, maternal labours that exist outside of dominant economies of labour and production, with critiques of intellectual labour economies that are present in immaterial labour discourse (Hardt 2007, pp. xi–xii). For sharing, affective labour signals the intensities and forces in strategies of 'expression, reception and exchange' (McCosker 2013, p. 15).

I draw attention to affective labours in enactments of sharing, and the ways in which they are performed, meaning the systems of rules and procedures that can be observed. By recognising distinct strategies, we can begin to develop a more detailed understanding of the way reciprocity functions in sharing practices and the way, through becoming routine, social norms emerge.

Labours of Reciprocity

When I asked Hana, a 36-year-old film studies lecturer at a Melbourne University, to tell me about her sharing practices she recounted a recent exchange on Facebook with a friend she'd previously met online in Yahoo! Answers. She and her friend were having a conversation about absurd song lyrics. The interaction itself was rather comedic and nonsensical and would have been even more so were it not for the labour of reciprocity both people invested in making the interaction meaningful:

> He put on this particular status update, 'Like this status update and I will attempt to tell your future through an 80s song'. So I liked it and he's popped onto my page on Facebook and he's written 'Gazes into the crystal coffee mug' and the lyrics for 'Shock the Monkey' to tell me the future. I'll read the lyrics: *'Fox the fox. Rat the rat. You can ape the ape, I know about that. There is one thing you must be sure of, I can't take any more. Darling, don't you monkey with the monkey. Monkey, monkey, monkey. Don't you know you're going to shock the monkey'*.[1] I liked it and he wrote 'the future cannot be changed.' So I wrote 'I've been banned from shocking monkeys' and he wrote 'then how are we to obtain the legendary electric monkeys?' And that was the end of the exchange.
>
> (Hana)

Several strategies of reciprocation were enacted in the exchange. For example, Hana paid attention to her friend's status update and consequently responded to it. Furthermore, their responses to one another were equally nonsensical; neither broke the theme of absurdity. When Hana was conversing with her friend on Facebook, he was not the only audience or recipient of her performance. The encounter was also shared with friends who could see her Facebook page, friends who could see his Facebook page and mutual friends who could see both pages. Indeed, one specific phenomenon of digital culture is this folding together of various social networks within interfaces such as Facebook (Wesch 2009). Specifically recognizing those who may encounter the conversation, a reciprocal other is identified in Hana's friend's initial status update which anticipates a response, if not several, to his proposition: 'Like this status update and I will attempt to tell *your* future through an 80s song' (Hana, emphasis mine).

Additionally, through their interaction Hana and her friend demonstrated their relationship to one another, showing themselves to be online contacts who were intimately aware of each other's sense of humour. Their interaction also performed familiarity of and taste in a particular genre of music. The song lyrics shared in their banter were many years old; Hana recollected the memories invoked by the particular song they discussed, linking the performance of the encounter with previous presentations of self.

Hana acknowledges that the conversation is particular to the relationship she and her friend developed in Yahoo! Answers, and that she was unlikely to have a similar type of nonsensical conversation with other friends on Facebook:

> We have a very similar, weird sense of humour. There are a handful of friends that I met on Yahoo Answers, we met because we used to hang out in a very silly part of Yahoo Answers and answer questions ridiculously posed of ourselves . . . There'd be other friends of mine who'd get it and others who wouldn't appreciate it so much . . . While I wouldn't necessarily be posting lyrics to 80s songs all over their pages, I think they would appreciate the sentiment or sense of humour.
>
> (Hana)

While anyone with access to the initial status update and consequential conversation might engage or react, the content is specific enough that it obstructs casual reciprocation. Hana imagines that there would be few of her friends who would 'get' the joke, and she assumes the majority of her Facebook friends will dismiss the exchange, without the desire to reciprocate or intervene.

As this example from my data shows, the reciprocal audience is anticipated in a variety of ways. Hana's scenario raises awareness of the expectations, obligations and limitations of reciprocity in sharing practices.

Strategies of Reciprocity

Equivalence

Sharing requires an intended end point. Strategies of reciprocity are forms of engagement with, and reactions to, sharing practices. One assumption of sharing that emerges in the cultural imaginary is that sharing begets sharing in return, that is, tit for tat (Axelrod and Hamilton 1981; Axelrod 1984). People are culturally oriented to reciprocate based on a moral norm of how one ought to respond (Gouldner 1960). Morals norms of reciprocity also hold expectations of trust in the other person— to respond accordingly. For example, confessing or admitting personal feelings can evoke a response of similar sentiment. Lisa, a 28-year-old

engineer, discovered this when she admitted to being overwhelmed by the
expectations of a particular social group:

> In this hiking group, if someone's having an issue it's not ever dis-
> cussed. It's always about the next adventure or how the last adven-
> ture was. There are a couple of girls that recently I've been talking to
> a bit more. I've found that they're struggling with a few things and I
> just had no idea because everyone puts on brave faces. Because we do
> have to, there can't be any sort of weakness. You've got to hold your
> own. If there's someone who admits weakness or who can't carry
> their pack, then the rest of the group talk negatively about those
> people. So you never want to be that person who says 'I can't carry
> my pack, it's too heavy'.
>
> (Lisa)

When Lisa confessed to certain members of her walking group that she
was finding the walking courses challenging, several other companions
admitted the same thing. Until that moment Lisa had felt, as one of the
few females in the hiking group, she needed to be 'manly and macho'
(Lisa). Aware of problematic attitudes within the group towards gender,
she was uncomfortable voicing her concerns whenever she felt overwhelmed
by the demands of the physical activities. The formation of the group
meant that the women rarely spent time alone together, and so they turned
to email and Facebook to discuss the attitudes of their male counterparts
and their unwillingness to be viewed as 'weak'. They agreed that their
actions, and inactions, were contributing to the overall mentality of the
group. For instance, if a female group member fell behind, rather than
wait for her, they would continue ahead, not wanting to also fall behind.
When Lisa shared her experiences of the group with the other female
members, they, too, shared their own experiences, which she felt established a common bond amongst them. This caused them to each shift
their own practices within the group in order to be more supportive of
one another. Lisa shared her personal feelings about her position within
the group with the expectation that by doing so she might encourage
others to reciprocate. Lisa relies on normative expectations that, when a
person shares intimate details, they will be reciprocated by either similarly intimate details or a suitable emotional response (Gouldner 1960).
Reciprocation is an important means of social capital production in that
it allows individuals to develop 'trust and affective bonds' (Molm 2010,
p. 126). Reciprocation through equivalence is also present in online communities such as blogging communities (Gaudeul and Peroni 2010) and
file sharing (Giesler 2006) where it is a motivator for user contribution
(Wellman and Gulia 1999).

Reciprocity plays a transformative role in oversharing. Moments of
purposeful vulnerability as described earlier carry a longing for reciprocity

through equivalent sharing. Where such reciprocity is encountered, the person's oversharing is recognised and redeemed as affective intensity. In forms of moral panic, oversharing is often framed as a lack of awareness of social norms; however, most participants are very and alert to when they are divulging more details than their interlocutor. Without reciprocity, anxiety creeps in. For instance, 19-year-old student Esel describes her anxiety over uneven sharing practices within a close friendship, which contradicts her expectations of reciprocity. Now at a different university to her best friend from school, she shares mostly via phone calls and messenger:

> I share everything with my best friend. She doesn't share anything with me. It's hard to share everything when she doesn't really share that much. I guess its kind of annoying because you're giving so much but you're not getting anything in return.
>
> (Esel)

Identifying such challenges to the boundaries of disclosure illustrates how the social norms of sharing are continually being negotiated.

A continual lack of equivalence of sharing practices can undermine relationships and instil feelings of resentment because this contravenes normative expectations. A lack of reciprocation over extended periods causes relationships to be less stable (Hallinan 1978). Esel is frustrated by the uneven balance in her relationship with her best friend. She persists with sharing with her friend in the hope that her friend will eventually reciprocate, but, as time goes on, she feels more frustrated with the lack of reciprocity and starts to doubt the friendship: 'I don't know if I trust her anymore, so I guess I don't tell her everything' (Esel).

Considerations of Consequences

Strategies of reciprocation are more than simply 'like for like'. Reciprocity can maintain the momentum of sharing practices in onward, dispersed actions, through a process of cause and effect, as a 'symbol of relation' (Lawler and Yoon 1996, p. 91). Such consequential acts are initiated by a performance of sharing, itself motivated by the expectation of consequence. By way of illustration, Nancy Baym discusses considerations of consequences as strategies of causality in 'The Swedish Model', a network of independent music labels who gift music files to fans in anticipation of recirculation, 'building audience, community, and endowing the music with credibility' (2011, p. 31).

Although expectations of consequence play a role in determining which sharing practices will be performed, consequences of sharing are not always foreseen, intended or known to the performer. For example, Heather, a 27-year-old accountant, describes how her expectations of consequences influenced her sharing practices on her blog. Heather spent, she felt, an inordinate amount of time discussing her close friend Naomi's personal state of affairs with very little time given to her own. After a particularly lengthy and typical phone call, she wanted to draw attention to this:

> After I hung up, I realised that she hadn't asked anything about how I was or asked about the fact that I was at home by myself while my husband's away for a few months. She hasn't asked how I was going, or any of that sort of stuff. My blog post that day was an attempt to guilt Naomi into calling me and asking me how I'm going, but it didn't work.
>
> (Heather)

Knowing that her friend Naomi subscribed to her blog, Heather wrote an exaggerated blog post hoping her friend would be spurred into sympathetic realisation and would call her back. In the interview, Heather bitterly revealed that the blog post was, in fact, ineffective and, worse, led to certain family members teasing her for the melodramatic, and uncharacteristic outpouring of self-pity.

As Heather's family reminded her, there are 'normal' expectations of what should be shared. Intentionally acting outside of these expectations can be a provocation for reciprocity. For instance, Clare frequently acts outside of other's expectations of what she will share on Facebook in order to provoke a response:

> I found a photo coming up in my Facebook of some other person but it was labelled as me. I thought that was pretty funny so I took that as my profile photo for a few weeks and really confused a whole bunch of people. I do a whole lot of that silly stuff, like I put 'engaged to a Vulcan' which really got a lot of people interested.
>
> (Clare)

By 'mucking around' with her Facebook profile, Clare endeavours to ensure consequences for her sharing. She does not expect that others will follow her example and alter their own profiles; instead, she imagines that it will prompt others to contact her, thereby constructing an opportunity for social engagement.

'Sociability' is one of the key purposes of online interactions (Preece 2000; Baker 2012). Goals of specific performances of sociability are linked to the identities of the people involved and their relationship to one another (Baym 1995; Katz et al. 2004). When we spoke, Esel was grappling with what consequences her sharing practices may have for her close friend. She was aware of a change of behaviour in her friend and was concerned that these changes pointed to an eating disorder. Aware of this possibility, she admirably researched online for how to deal with a friend in such a predicament and found advice that related specifically to her own sharing practices:

> I think my friend's bulimic, my best friend, so I've been reading what I should do—how I should act around her and apparently, you're not supposed to talk about weight, or people's appearances. You're meant to say 'doesn't that person have such a nice smile' or 'isn't that person's personality great' instead of 'look how skinny or look how fat that person is' or 'I wish I was that skinny' or 'oh gosh I need to lose a lot of weight'. Apparently, a lot of that stuff leads to eating disorders so from now on I'm going to stop sharing that kind of stuff with her. I say that stuff without even thinking, you know—'I really need to lose some weight'.
>
> (Esel)

Esel is acutely aware of limiting the boundaries of what she shares given the context of her friend's condition. She brings a different register of awareness to her sharing practices based on their relationship and recognises the potential for her own sharing practices affecting her friend's well-being.

Sharing practices are performed with the intention of initiating particular consequences and avoiding others within the contextual and temporal boundaries of particular social relationships (Goffman 1959). This draws attention to the idealised role of affect in performances of sharing (Baym 2011, p. 37), in which 'there will be an ongoing and generalised indebtedness, gratitude, expectation, memory, sentiment—in short, lively, social feeling' (Mifsud 2007, p. 84). For example, Judith Donath (2007) identifies that sharing and reciprocation are connected with the commitment to social relationship maintenance, and Jessa Lingel and Mor Naaman (2012) find that reciprocation through commenting and posting additional content to videos posted on YouTube are expressions of attentiveness and reputation management. For my participants, considerations of consequences indicate the commitment to social relationships and attentiveness to other's needs.

Listening

The first process of reciprocity is equivalence, and the second is the consideration of consequences. The third process of reciprocity, listening, relies upon both of these processes. Listening captures all means of engagement and reactions by which a practice of sharing is recognised. As a necessary condition and precursor to other strategies of reciprocity, listening is an important formalisation in the process of reciprocity yet as a practice it is often downplayed or overlooked (Lacey 2013). Few consider the importance of listening for sharing. Crawford (2009) identifies that those more often referred to as lurkers make up the majority of many online communities, but that the term *lurking* implies a marginal, non-contributive, stigmatized presence, which is at odds with an active contribution through receptiveness (2009, p. 527). Others have also recognised the importance of lurkers to online communities (Nonnecke and Preece 2003; Lee, Chen and Jiang 2006). *Listeners*, Crawford argues, is a better term than *lurkers* because it indicates an active and necessary position for the communication process. Listening is also a better register of presence (Couldry 2006).

Performances of sharing position others as potential listeners. For example, while overseas Clare wrote a blog to share her travelling stories with her friends. She gained comfort from this activity even though she was unable to identify whom, if any, of her friends read it:

> When I went to Turkey, because I was travelling on my own, I decided to create a blog. Travelling on your own is really lonely. When I got on my blog I felt like I was talking to my friends. I could put stuff up, put pictures up and share stuff. I didn't feel like I was on my own anymore. I didn't even get many comments. Maybe they weren't checking the blog but I did have a lot of hits which was interesting.
>
> (Clare)

Clare used her blog to communicate with her friends and relieve her feelings of loneliness while she was travelling by constructing a sense of presence. Reciprocation constitutes presence through the anticipation of listening. As Esther Milne describes,

> [p]resence is a term that need not always refer to *material, corporeal* presence. Rather, presence is an effect achieved in communication (whether by letters, postcards, or email, for example) when interlocutors imagine the psychological or, sometimes, physical presence of the other.
>
> (2010, p. 2)

At the time Clare was writing her blog posts, she had no idea whether they might be read, but the possibility that there might be listeners motivated her to share her stories. She wasn't put off by the lack of comments because she didn't view comments as the only form of engagement with her writing. While the blog interface recorded and displayed the number of visits to her page (known as hits), she did not consider this to be definitively indicative of her reaching her intended audience. It was only when she returned home that Clare found confirmation of engagements with her blog. She discovered that she was asked very little about her trip in general; instead, people referred to particular elements of her blog posts and asked her to elaborate with more specific details. This greatly pleased her as she felt the blog avoided the banality of repeating the basic details of her trip many times over. While the possibility of others listening to her blog was sufficient motivation for her to share at the time, consequences of that listening further affirmed that sharing. Through later reciprocal actions, Clare was able to broadly quantify reciprocation of her blogging. More generally, quantifying listening is problematic. It is not enough to simply count those who may listen, as counting listeners does not allow for variations in labours of listening.

Listening requires immaterial and affective labour. It requires immaterial labour in the sense that it requires actual attention and affective labour of 'human contact and interaction' (Hardt and Negri 2000, p. 290). Esel demonstrates the 'reciprocal, embodied nature of listening' (Couldry 2006, p. 6):

> I'm happy to listen because I think other people may need to share their problems with somebody or it will just build up. Like my friend, she won't tell me anything. All her problems are built-up into an eating disorder.
>
> (Esel)

Esel attempts to make clear her willingness to listen in an effort to get her friend to share. If sharing requires an intended end point, then demonstrating the existence of such an end point encourages future sharing practices and establishes a means of stabilising or strengthening the relationship.

Importantly, sharing needs be received, and the receipt of the sharing itself shared (Wittkower 2013). Therefore, Clare constructs the possibility of presence in her travels, experiencing the object—which in her case is the actual travel, not the blog post about the experience—with the future possible ideal of the experience being shared. On reading her blog, her friends and family affirm her hopes of sharing her experiences and later their responses provide further affirmation. Such constructions of shared experience through retroactive reciprocity can be disruptive. As with other forms of oversharing, some might not welcome being positioned in the shared experience. Similarly, an unintended receiver may, through reciprocation, be retroactively co-present in the experience against the desires of the sharer.

Legibility and Provocations

Charles Husband draws attention to important distinctions between listening and understanding:

> Listening, it seems to me, is an act of attention, a willingness to focus on the other, to heed both their presence and their communication.

It is only a necessary precursor to understanding. . . . Understanding, on the other hand, is an act of empathetic comprehension, a willing searching after the other's intention and message.

(2009, p. 441)

Listening requires attentiveness for there to be understanding, but understanding is also conditional on comprehensibility. A person may, perhaps unintentionally, perform sharing in such a way that others cannot understand. Sharing in a way that can be understood requires some extra effort. For instance, Jason describes the difficulties of writing emails that will be efficiently informative in their reception: 'It can cause problems if people aren't listening properly. Listening means reading the email properly' (Jason). Jason spends a considerable amount of time constructing his emails in an attempt to limit the number of emails required for work-related negotiations: 'Because I want to get everything over in one email rather than twenty one-liners back and forth, back and forth, back and forth. I find that really annoying'. He does this to avoid what he sees as the tiresomeness of email exchange: 'It can get a bit tedious, the constant email back and forth, trying to get the message across' (Jason). Jason works to make the meaning of his message clear, but even with this effort, the exchange often requires several iterations. He is frustrated by the lack of labour invested by the recipient in reading the email closely for interpretation and comprehension.

Understanding is not automatic; it requires interpretative labour. Expectations of what kind of labour will be invested in interpretation shape their construction. For example, Christopher, 37-year-old web designer, has come to know that particular work associates act on information shared in the first section of an email and overlook the remainder. To manage this, he has developed a particular way of sharing knowledge with them via email:

> I send Zuresh separate emails because like Sally, he reads the first bit and disregards the second bit. You can't write part one, part two, part three and have him go through and address things. I know he doesn't work that way because I send him stuff to do and he does the first thing and sends it back and I say what about the second thing and he goes 'what second thing'? It's not uncommon.
>
> (Christopher)

If Christopher has a number of remarks or requests, he needs to send these as separate emails because Zuresh and Sally only respond to the first enquiry in the body of the email. This confounds the notion of being able to share complex, detailed information via email. Christopher needs to simplify the email content by dividing it into less detailed sections, which are sent as individual emails at some time apart.

Participants also try to reduce the amount of labour required in email correspondence by limiting the quantity of detail shared. For instance, Shimon avoids giving his family much information about his day-to-day life because it may result in further, more detailed emails:

> I share with family, but if they're not within close vicinity I tend to be a little bit more reserved. Mainly because I can't be arsed to write out a bloody long email to tell them what I've been up to, so I'll tell them the basics of what I've seen and things, but their overall knowledge of what's going on is probably a small percentage of what is actually going on. So the people I am sharing closely with are the people that live with me and my close friends and probably my co-workers.
>
> (Shimon)

Shimon shares the more profound details of his life with those he sees often face-to-face rather than those he is emotionally close with because his more intimate relationships with family, are often mediated by email. This requires a considerable effort on his behalf to convey the full affective details, whereas his communication with friends, housemates and co-workers is partially a consequence of their proximity to him. Conveying affective meaning in email, as with other communicative mediums, including social media platforms, requires labour, and there are considerable risks of being misinterpreted.

Similarly, a practice that is not intended as sharing may be interpreted as such by another. Understanding cannot be fixed, nor limited in its impact: 'Understanding is a process, and as such it is a catalyst that actively, even dangerously, interacts and changes whatever it comes into contact with' (Husband 2009, p. 443). For example, Darryl, when describing sharing, includes overhearing other people's phone conversations: 'even if they're not talking directly to me, they're still sharing a story or they're sharing information' (Darryl). Because Darryl can understand the significance of the conversation, he feels that he has participated in the sharing even though he is not a participant in the conversation. Social norms around eavesdropping and privacy prevent him from acting on that understanding.

Unintended audiences, such as those in the earlier examples, raise expectations of reciprocity and anxiety over a lack of reciprocity. Being the unwitting audience to another person's oversharing can also provoke anxiety because it locates people in an uncomfortable situation where they may feel obliged to reciprocate. Reciprocation in sharing can be seen as a process of endorsement and affirmation, so reciprocation of oversharing can be strategically performed in order to convey disapproval to the oversharer. James, an 18-year-old who had recently finished high school, describes how he observes this:

> If someone [posted a Facebook] status that was somehow perceived to be really day to day, mundane or not really interesting or not worth

sharing on Facebook—whatever that means, anyone can post whatever they want supposedly—others make a comment like 'cool story
bro' or they'd make some sort of smart-arsed sarcastic comment.

(James)

James witnesses group judgement of undesired sharing practices which
function to shame and humiliate the offender, and serve as a warning
to others. In conjunction with the affordances of the interface, there are
social conventions that are strongly enforced through reciprocation tactics. Reciprocity here is used as a form of social control to reinforce the
desired social norms of the group.

In identifying equivalence, consequence and listening as strategies of
reciprocity, together with processes of enforcing norms, labour is manifest. First, listening is a form of immaterial labour in that it requires
deliberate attention that is difficult to quantify (Crawford 2009). Second,
understanding is an additional immaterial labour required for any form
of equivalence, consequence or norming to occur, for without an understanding of sharing there can be no reciprocity (Husband 2009). Finally,
these strategies require that each interlocutor engages in affective labour,
by which feelings of ease or unease, excitement or indifference, calmness
or duress are experienced.

Expectations

The nature of the relationship between people affects the desire to reciprocate, and the specificity of labour invested: 'Naomi just talks to me
on the phone. I don't really get a word in. She just talks so I don't really
have to say much' (Heather). Although Heather is annoyed by her friend
Naomi's self-interest and lack of reciprocity (as discussed previously),
this aspect of uneven communication can also relieve her of pressure to
reciprocate. Conversely, she is comfortable talking to her grandmother
because her grandmother always has plenty to talk about and relieves
Heather of the pressure to share:

> We have this thing where I always say 'have you seen any good movies
> lately?' Because she goes to the movies with her friends once or twice
> a week so she'll always say 'oh I saw this and it was rubbish and I
> walked out and blah blah blah'. We always do that, that's our thing.
> (Heather)

Over time Heather and her grandmother have established topics of conversation, which means that she has expectations of how phone conversations will unfold. Also, should the conversation stall she has a repertoire
of familiar topics she can draw on and expect a response to. These practices of sharing form Heather's relationship with her grandmother. As

identified in the literature on social theories of sharing, these practices develop and form part of how each person is known to the other.

Meeting new people often means making oneself momentarily vulnerable, in order for each party to get to know one another and establish a connection. At the time of our interview, Esel had recently started at university and had spent much of the past few weeks getting to know new people:

> I've only just met them so what I'm sharing is about myself, like how my family is made up and where I live. They always want to know the basic 'about you' questions when they're trying to figure out what type of person you are.
>
> (Esel)

Similarly, Darryl describes how personal contact details are gradually shared when he is online dating:

> Online dating starts off extremely controlled, you don't know someone's email until the time you're comfortable sharing that. Then when you know their email you have an opportunity to get their phone number so you might start texting. I'd be happy to give someone my email straight away if they were interested in chatting but that's not always the case. I know a lot of people don't think like that, so it tends not to happen.
>
> (Darryl)

When I asked him the decisive factors for progressively sharing more personal details, he said, 'Longevity, knowing someone, a willingness of both parties to continue getting to know someone for whatever reason' (Darryl). For the relationship to progress, one person must tentatively push the boundary of disclosures and wait to see if their actions are reciprocated. If reciprocated, the relationship dynamic shifts towards being a fraction more intimate. This process happens many times over, each act of reciprocation extending the relationship further.

To give another example, Jose uses expectations of reciprocity to develop familiarity and social connectedness within his professional relationships. He shares sufficient personal information with his clients to develop a good rapport and to enable them to see him as somebody they can engage with. Jose acts the part of extending his relationship with them; however, he does not confuse where this boundary actually lies. He shares only sufficient details about his personal life to leverage better working relationships:

JOSE: I'm actually pretty social in my professional life because I want the clients to feel like I am their friend even though I'm not.

INTERVIEWER: How do you do that?
JOSE: By being open to them about normal stuff, letting them see me joking around.

Jose uses a similar strategy to develop better working relationships with his employees. He does this by being open in terms of what personal information he shares with them in order to encourage them to reciprocate by also being open:

> I like them to feel that I am their friend so if anything happens they can talk to me as a friend. It has definitely come in handy sometimes, such as when they are not happy with the client or something like that they will talk to me as a friend. I am able to act on matters a lot quicker because of that.
>
> (Jose)

Jose uses boundaries and expectations of reciprocity strategically to develop better working relationships with clients by enacting social intensification. It is unclear whether his clients are being quite so strategic, or if his actions would be considered by them to be manipulative.

Esel, as a 19-year-old moving into new social environments, was especially conscious of shifting social norms within her peer groups. Her interview emphasised the ongoing reflexive and sometimes contradictory processes that all my participants engaged in as they navigated devices, contexts, relationships and expectations when sharing. The balance between sharing and reciprocity is often fragile, subjective and even arbitrary. To prevent overstepping boundaries, people try to anticipate limits. For example, Esel is aware that information about her travels or thrilling adventures might be viewed by others as oversharing:

> I feel like people don't really want to hear everything that you've done, that's why I hold back. I think they just get bored. I guess when you've done stuff that other people haven't had an opportunity to do it feels like bragging all the time.
>
> (Esel)

Esel keeps from oversharing (or 'bragging' as she calls it) because she thinks it is a form of vanity. Such confessions show how subjects are aware of, and continually negotiating, boundaries and potential vulnerabilities.

Esel reads oversharing as vanity, 'wanting to shout out loud about one's uniqueness' (Agger 2012, p. 4): 'It is difficult to read oversharing as anything but narcissism, a projection of the self onto others' (Agger 2012, p. 7). Agger goes so far as to label oversharing as featuring elements of personality disorders, and being technologically determined:

Oversharing means to divulge more of their inner feelings, opinions, and sexuality than they would in person, or even over the phone. Text messaging, Facebooking, tweeting, camming, blogging, online dating, and Internet porn are vehicles of this oversharing which blurs the boundaries between public and private life.

(Agger 2012, p. xi)

Yet, counter to Agger's argument that oversharing is a technological phenomenon, Esel and other participants indicate that it is not just on social media or through mobile devices that people are confused by how to negotiate intimate boundaries. Across many contexts boundaries of reciprocity can coexist, converge and, at times, conflict. Jose recalls an incident when a client gave him an expensive gift which he felt was unacceptable under the circumstances in which they knew one another:

One of my clients wanted to get personal with me, in a relationship, when I was then with my partner. The client kept trying to give me gifts and I told her 'no, I have a partner. It's just business with you'. She couldn't understand why I wouldn't accept any gifts. She got me a watch. That is a big gift, and not just that, she got me other stuff. That sort of sharing in my professional life is not acceptable.

(Jose)

Jose had developed a close working relationship with a female client, who had attempted to transform the relationship into something more personal by gifting him personal items. Jose did not want to respond in kind to her gift as he wished to maintain the relationship on a professional level and needed to articulate his boundaries to the client. Often, boundaries to reciprocity are not so easily substantiated. For this reason, moments of overstepping boundaries can be fraught with tension and confusion.

As Jose demonstrates, sharing is not always reciprocated or desired. Experiences of sharing, as represented in my interviews, reveal opposing and conflicting desires at odds with the 'motherhood' statements of sharing discussed in Chapter 1. For instance, Michelle, a 35-year-old personal trainer, stated,

I've got a friend called Alice. Alice often calls me and she does all the talking and I just listen and say 'hmm-hmm', 'ah right', 'hmmm', 'ohhhh'. I get stories about what she had for breakfast and what the two boys had for breakfast about six weeks ago, and I don't really need to know what they had for breakfast six weeks ago, you know. But recently she hasn't been calling me much which is kind of a relief.

(Michelle)

Michelle takes the calls from her friend because she wants to hear from her and it is their primary way of staying in contact. She would prefer, however, that the conversations varied, that they weren't so banal and that she had more opportunities to contribute to the conversation. Assigned the role of listener, she feels that the balance of sharing in their relationship is unequal. Sharing practices locate individuals in particular positions in each encounter. Michelle is located as listener in her encounters with Alice, a consequence of repetition throughout the history of their friendship. She is expected to reciprocate by listening, and so she feels obliged to comply in order to maintain the friendship.

Expectations of reciprocation in sharing practices are especially apparent when reciprocity is absent. For example, Addison, a 22-year-old online content manager, is incredibly uncomfortable when she finds herself in a predicament where she has shared and is waiting to see if her sharing is going to be reciprocated:

> I don't like it at all. I hate it! I just think they're not going to share anything back with me. At a later date they can go away and tell everybody what a dickhead I was, and I can't tell anybody they're also a dickhead because I have no idea about them.
>
> (Addison)

In moments prior to or in absence of reciprocated sharing, Addison fears that she has made herself vulnerable by oversharing. She has anticipated that her own vulnerability will be mirrored: 'If I'm going to go into gory details, I also expect you to tell me some of your gory details' (Addison). In such circumstances, reciprocity is a mutually protective social mechanism. It uncovers the risk and vulnerability of sharing. Going into 'gory details' involves momentary oversharing. Brief moments of oversharing are a means of testing and pushing the limits of a relationship in the hope of deepening or intensifying it. This form of purposeful vulnerability is at odds with what Agger (2012) positions as frank disregard of social norms that he associates with oversharing.

Imaginations

In the forms of oversharing discussed so far, the people involved in the exchange are known to each other. A more ambiguous situation arises on digital platforms with an imagined audience. On many social media platforms, connections are reciprocal, and users, even when not explicitly connected to one another are designated 'friends', and at least are aware of who is following them. While friend lists and privacy settings write an audience 'into being' (boyd 2007), they are imprecise in defining that audience at any given moment. Furthermore, depending on the site and privacy settings, such lists are not necessarily indicative of total audience size. Second, although explicitly connected, social media interfaces allow users to hide certain activities from view or block another person's updates. Also, patterns of use are distinct, with people spending variable amounts of time on the platform across different devices so that users cannot always be sure who has seen their post or when. Participants therefore navigate multiple vulnerabilities when sharing. To manage these variables and to reduce feelings of risk and vulnerability borne of the unknown, participants construct an imagined audience (Marwick and boyd 2011) using cues from the interface and social contexts (boyd 2007). For instance, Esel likes to post song lyrics as her Facebook status:

> I'll be listening to a song and I'll usually post the lyrics that are applicable to my life. I think a lot of people wouldn't be 'Oh, this is what's going on in her life'. They just think 'oh she probably likes the song', you know. I'm not really giving that much information.
>
> (Esel)

While Esel places particular significance on the lyrics she posts as her status update, she imagines an unresponsive, inattentive audience. Sharing her most private thoughts and feelings through song lyrics, a common practice described by Marwick and boyd (2011) as social steganography, she imagines few people, if any, will identify the personal significance of the lyrics to her. She uses this strategy as a protective mechanism, satisfying her desire to share while protecting herself from the effects of vulnerability through over-disclosure and non-reciprocity. Like Marwick and boyd's participants, Esel is uncomfortable with locating herself in relation to an active audience. As Marwick and boyd note,

> [w]hat emerges here is not that these individuals lack an audience, but that they are uncomfortable labelling interlocutors and witnesses as an 'audience'. In bristling over the notion of audience, they are likely rejecting a popularly discussed act of 'personal branding' as running counter to what they value: authenticity. In other words, consciously speaking to an audience is perceived as inauthentic.
>
> (2011, p. 119)

Rather than conceive of herself crafting an image or brand, Esel considers herself to be 'authentically unique' (Grazian 2003). Posting song lyrics is a practice Esel regularly engages with. She imagines herself to be unique in the way she uses them to present self:

> Other people don't do that I don't think. A few of my friends do but they are just doing it because they like the song. And I only know that because I know those people.
>
> (Esel)

Esel separates her own motivations for sharing from those of her friends. Identifying her own practices as being motivated by deep, reflexive thinking is also a protective strategy. By imagining that other people's song lyric posts are not worth 'reading into', she also imagines that other people will not look too deeply at hers, if they read them at all:

> I'm not really concerned about it. I think my close friends or these people from high school all have their own lives going on as well . . . I don't think they really care what is going on, on my page. I can't imagine them being like 'I'll just check what's going on with this girl's page on Facebook'.
>
> (Esel)

Yet later in the interview, Esel mentions that she is concerned that people might read her Facebook posts closely and might make judgements about her based on them:

> Especially the skanks back in high school. I started deleting them all because I can just see them all judging me. They probably don't even read my posts but it just feels like because they can see it . . . I definitely limit what I am saying.
>
> (Esel)

In fascinating tension, Esel cannot imagine anyone reading her Facebook posts too closely, yet at the same time, she self-monitors in case they do. While she realises that old high school friends probably have other priorities than reading her Facebook posts, she still imagines them as an audience to her self-presentation. Esel imagines these audiences and undertakes protective self-monitoring. However, Esel fluctuates between imagining the 'ideal reader', one who will take her song lyrics at face value and leave her emotions concealed, and the 'nightmare reader' (Marwick and boyd 2011, p. 125), who will condemn her for her personal revelations. As Marwick and boyd note,

> [c]ontext collapse creates an audience that is often imagined as its most sensitive members: parents, partners, and bosses. This 'nightmare reader' is the opposite of the ideal reader and may limit personal disclosure.
>
> (2011, p. 125)

Esel constructs both these imagined audiences in her sharing practices.

It is not possible to predict what another may interpret in what is shared. There can be considerable fallout when interpretations clash with intentions, or when contexts collapse. An example is what Addison refers to as the 'lava lamp incident'. While working in a marketing role, she posted on her own Facebook status her dislike of lava lamps because as lamps, they give out little light. A colleague saw the post and told another colleague (not on Facebook), who happened to have a lava lamp in her office, what Addison had written. Both colleagues felt that the post was aimed at the lava lamp owner and told their manager about the status update. Addison was severely reprimanded over her personal use of social media, even though the comment had been on her personal profile and had not been directed towards her colleague. Since the 'lava lamp incident' Addison is extremely cautious about what she posts on Facebook and omits strong personal opinions as well as anything that may be construed negatively, although she admits it is impossible to categorically identify what might be interpreted. Addison's imagined audience represents the 'nightmare reader', overly sensitive and demanding careful monitoring of personal disclosures. Many social networks and self-interests converge on platforms such as Facebook, in which sharing practices can be specifically targeted. Addison also posts links on her Facebook page from her blog, which is focused on feminist issues arising in popular culture. While many of her Facebook friends are aware of her blog, not all of them share her activist stance on feminist matters. Rather than leverage her professional profile on Facebook, she limits expressing opinions her unenlightened Facebook friends might find controversial. Instead, she redirects those who are interested in such topics to her blog, where she is more willing to engage in heated debate. Addison shows awareness of the nuances of particular audiences and modulates her sharing practices accordingly. She limits her exposure to unintended audiences who might interpret her posts of personal feminist struggles as oversharing by creating links to her blog on Facebook and transferring the labour of clicking through to her blog posts onto those who choose to be her audience.

In addition to imagined collapsed audiences, which audiences sharing is explicitly intended for, are also considered strategically. For instance, Philip particularly likes to share links to music on Facebook: 'I'm really avidly into music so I like to share links to YouTube videos of songs or music videos that I like and send those around to people' (Philip). As the event organiser of a monthly nightclub event, Philip shares most of the links he posts to a Facebook page set up for this event:

> I have a Facebook group for this monthly event and I'll post links to YouTube videos of music that much of the audience wouldn't be familiar with but might be interested in. One of the reasons I do that is that it gives them a good preview of some of the music that's played at the night.
>
> (Philip)

Philip shares these links to demonstrate his knowledge of the particular genre featured at the event, a practice which also reinforces Philip's status as the event organiser. Sharing links to the group's Facebook page or posting them to the profile pages of friends associated with the group, Philip selectively presents himself in a professional context, specifically to those who might further his career. To his closest friends on Facebook, he rarely posts music, although they are aware of his music interests. Instead, he is more likely to post links to articles, images and comics that he finds funny or interesting. Each of these activities demonstrates his awareness of the frameworks of social acceptance. Philip mobilises particular sharing practices for particular relationships; each presentation of self is framed by the role(s) he takes on in these networks. Roles structure what presentations of self are acceptable (Goffman 1959), while audiences can be conceptualised and navigated for specific purposes through sharing practices.

Conclusion

In this chapter, I argued that reciprocity is a necessary possibility for sharing and an important means of establishing and maintaining social relationships. Strategies of reciprocation include equivalence, where expectations of trust are enacted through corresponding sharing; consequence, where reciprocity indicates a commitment to social relationships and a desire to meet another's needs; and listening, which registers presence and enactment of initial engagement. By unpacking each of these strategies I established the centrality of reciprocity to sharing. Furthermore, strategies of reciprocity elucidate the labour of sharing. Acts of anticipation, interpretation and understanding in sharing require immaterial labour, as well as affective labour in the emotional intensities of reception.

Additionally, this chapter showed that sharing is a process of making oneself vulnerable in anticipation of social intensification and argued that such vulnerability is productive for negotiating and establishing social norms. As I established in the previous chapter, sharing is an evolving social norm. Exploring the circumstances of reciprocity highlights some of the ways that social norms of sharing are evolving, for example, in practices of oversharing whereby limits of social acceptability are tested and enacted, often through technological affordances. In the next chapter I examine how technological affordances are intimately connected with sharing practices.

Note

1. This is a reference to the song 'Shock the Monkey' by Peter Gabriel, which was released through Geffen Records in 1982.

References

Agger, B 2012, *Oversharing: Presentations of self in the internet age*, Routledge, New York, NY.

Arendt, H 2013, *The human condition*, University of Chicago Press, Chicago, IL.

Axelrod, RM 1984, *The evolution of cooperation*, Basic Books, New York, NY.

Axelrod, RM and Hamilton, WD 1981, 'The evolution of cooperation', *Science*, vol. 211, no. 4489, pp. 1390–1396.

Baker, A 2012, 'The exchange of material culture among rock fans in online communities', *Information, Communication & Society*, vol. 15, no. 4, pp. 519–536.

Baym, N 1995, 'The emergence of community in computer-mediated communication', in M Smith and P Kollock (eds), *Communities in cyberspace*, Routledge, London, pp. 138–163.

Baym, N 2011, 'The Swedish model: Balancing markets and gifts in the music industry', *Popular Communication*, vol. 9, no. 1, pp. 22–38.

Bickford, S 1996, *The dissonance of democracy*, Cornell University Press, Ithaca, NY.

boyd, d 2007, 'Why youth <3 social network sites: The role of networked publics in teenage social life', in D Buckingham (ed), *Youth identity and digital media*, MIT Press, Cambridge, MA, pp. 119–142.

Cammaerts, B 2011, 'Disruptive sharing in a digital age: Rejecting neoliberalism?', *Continuum: Journal of Media & Cultural Studies*, vol. 25, no. 1, pp. 47–62.

Couldry, N 2006, *Listening beyond the echoes: Media, ethics, and agency in an uncertain world*, Paradigm Press, Boulder, CO.

Couldry, N 2009, 'Rethinking the politics of voice: Commentary', *Continuum: Journal of Media & Cultural Studies*, vol. 23, no. 4, pp. 579–582.

Crawford, K 2009, 'Following you: Disciplines of listening in social media', *Continuum: Journal of Media & Cultural Studies*, vol. 23, no. 4, pp. 525–535.

Donath, J 2007, 'Signals in social supernets', *Journal of Computer-Mediated Communication*, vol. 13, no. 1, pp. 231–251.

Gaudeul, A and Peroni, C 2010, 'Reciprocal attention and norm of reciprocity in blogging networks', *Jena Economic Research Papers*, vol. 20, pp. 1–19.

Giesler, M 2006, 'Consumer gift systems', *Journal of Consumer Research*, vol. 33, no. 2, pp. 283–290.

Goffman, E 1959, *The presentation of self in everyday life*, Anchor Books, New York, NY.

Gouldner, AW 1960, 'The norm of reciprocity: A preliminary statement', *American Sociological Review*, vol. 25, pp. 161–178.

Grazian, D 2003, *Blue Chicago*, University of Chicago Press, Chicago, IL.

Hallinan, MT 1978, 'The process of friendship formation', *Social Networks*, vol. 1, no. 2, pp. 193–210.

Hardt, M 2007, 'Foreword: What affects are good for', in PT Clough, and J Halley (eds), *The affective turn: Theorizing the social*, Duke University Press, Durham, NC, pp. ix–xiii.

Hardt, M and Negri, A 2000, *Empire*, Harvard University Press, Cambridge, MA.

Heidegger, M 1962, *Being and time*, trans. J Macquarrie and E Robinson, Blackwell, Malden, MA.

Husband, C 2009, 'Between listening and understanding', *Continuum: Journal of Media & Cultural Studies*, vol. 23, no. 4, pp. 441–443.

Katz, J, Rice, R, Acord, S, Dasgupta, K and David, K 2004, 'Personal mediated communication and the concept of community in theory and practice', in P Kalbfleisch (ed), *Communication and community, communication yearbook*, vol. 28, Erlbaum, Mahwah, NJ, pp. 315–371.

Kennedy, J and Milne, E 2013, 'Public privacy: Reciprocity and silence', *PLATFORM: Journal of Media and Communication*, vol. 5, no. 1.

Lacey, K 2013, *Listening publics: The politics and experience of listening in the media age*, John Wiley & Sons, New York, NY.

Lawler, EJ and Yoon, J 1996, 'Commitment in exchange relations: Test of a theory of relational cohesion', *American Sociological Review*, vol. 61, no. 1, 89–108.

Lee, Y, Chen, F and Jiang, H 2006, 'Lurking as participation: A community perspective on lurkers' identity and negotiability', *Proceedings of the 7th international conference on learning sciences*, International Society of the Learning Sciences, Bloomington, IN, pp. 404–410.

Lingel, J and Naaman, M 2012, 'You should have been there, man: Live music, DIY content and online communities', *New Media & Society*, vol. 14, no. 2, pp. 332–349.

Marwick, AE and boyd, d 2011, 'I tweet honestly, I tweet passionately: Twitter users, context collapse, and the imagined audience', *New Media & Society*, vol. 13, no. 1, pp. 114–133.

McCosker, A 2013, *Intensive media: Aversive affect and visual culture*, Palgrave Macmillan, London.

Mifsud, M 2007, 'On rhetoric as gift/giving', *Philosophy and Rhetoric*, vol. 40, no. 1, pp. 89–107.

Milne, E 2010, *Letters, postcards, email: Technologies of presence*, Routledge, London.

Molm, LD 2010, 'The structure of reciprocity', *Social Psychology Quarterly*, vol. 73, no. 2, pp. 119–131.

Nonnecke, B and Preece, J 2003, 'Silent participants: Getting to know lurkers better', in *From usenet to CoWebs*, Springer, London, pp. 110–132.

Preece, J 2000, *Online communities: Designing usability, supporting sociability*, John Wiley & Sons Ltd, New York, NY.

Solove, D 2007, *The future of reputation: Gossip, rumour and privacy on the internet*, Yale University Press, New Haven, CT and London.

Tufekci, Z 2008, 'Can you see me now? Audience and disclosure regulation in online social network sites', *Bulletin of Science, Technology & Society*, vol. 28, no. 1, pp. 20–36.

Vallor, S 2012, 'Flourishing on Facebook: Virtue friendship and new social media', *Ethics and Information Technology*, vol. 14, no. 3, pp. 185–199.

Wellman, B and Gulia, M 1999, 'Virtual communities as communities: Net surfers don't ride alone', in P Kollock and M Smith (eds), *Communities in cyberspace*, Routledge, London, pp. 167–194.

Wesch, M 2009, 'YouTube and you: Experiences of self-awareness in the context collapse of the recording webcam', *Explorations in Media Ecology*, vol. 8, no. 2, pp. 19–34.

Wittkower, DE 2013, 'A phenomenology of SNS sharing', *Selected Papers of Internet Research*, vol. 14, pp. 1–3.

6   Intimate Technologies

Introduction

In the previous chapter I revealed the expectations and conditions of reciprocity for sharing, the role of the other in sharing, and the affective labours of sharing. Affect is located in both the relationships 'we establish *with* media devices, platforms and content', and '*through* them' (McCosker 2013, p. 20). This chapter looks specifically at the interplay between the materialities of technoculture and sharing practices. As identified in Chapter Two, this examination of socio-technical features is somewhat lacking in accounts of sharing in digital culture. I emphasise the intimacies of technologies in sharing practices, looking specifically at relationships to these technologies, how technologies mediate sharing practices and how individuals navigate affordances for mediation.

As with the previous two chapters, this chapter is organised into three distinct sections which address key aspects of materiality and technoculture. These aspects are organised by degrees of granularity, moving through micro, meso to macro interpretations of mediated affordances. I begin by discussing specific affordances, with particular attention given to email and the role this interface plays in mediating sharing. Next, I discuss the role of specific devices, using mobile phones as an example of how people navigate material affordances and perceptions of connectivity. Finally, I consider the broader contexts and 'networked publics' (boyd 2007, 2008, 2014) which mediate sharing because these help us understand performances of sharing.

Materialities

While much of the discussion in the preceding two chapters focuses on the sharing of immaterial and affective objects, materiality plays a key role in practices of sharing. Sharing performances are specific to the material affordances of media technologies.

Affordances are relational and can be seen as the perceived features that infer structure (Hogan 2009). Initially defined by James Gibson (1986), an ecological psychologist, as available features that provide the potential for action. A more nuanced definition is that affordances, actual or not, are perceived and indicate properties of use that are dependent on an individual's context (Norman 1988). Perception of affordances is relative to one's being-in-the world. Affordances are unevenly experienced, yet there are assumptions that everyone will experience them similarly. Furthermore, affordances of technologies are not inherently understood, and navigating and interpreting affordances requires material and affective labour.

Affordances are both technological and social. Digital culture offers a framework in which social affordances are understood as the cues a person perceives or accesses from their particular position within their network(s) according to their specific temporal-spatiality, relativity and information (Hogan 2009, pp. 30–40). Social affordances can be understood as who or what a person may interact with in a given time and space, how they might be connected to another person or object and what information is available to the person regarding this interaction.

Attending to the affordances of digital technologies is an important step in acknowledging the materiality of technoculture. Digital technologies are significant because of their symbolic values in material culture. Yet, as David Beer (2012) states, we need to attend to more than the functionality or affordances of technologies. We also need to consider the materiality of such devices and how people form attachments to them. He suggests thinking about media as 'objects that are intimately incorporated into routine bodily practices' (Beer 2012, p. 362). Beer traces attachment back to Walter Benjamin who, in relation to book collectors, argues it is not what the technology contains but the materiality of the technology that is of importance to the user. This reframe moves us away from what is being shared, such as the formats and scale of digitised content predominant in much of the literature discussed in Chapter 2. In material everyday life, this includes 'the objects that people hold in their hands, place in their pockets and bags and doc into their laptops and stereos—in short, the interfaces' (Beer 2012, p. 363).

Similarly material culture theorists address the significance of objects, arguing that they play a necessary cultural role. For example, Daniel Miller (2008, 2010) emphasises how objects are present in everyday routines, how owners have intimate relationships with objects, and how those objects mediate relationships with others. Arjun Appadurai also urges us to

> follow the things themselves, for their meanings are inscribed in their forms, their uses, their trajectories. It is only through the analysis of these trajectories that we can interpret the human transactions and calculations that enliven things. Thus, even though from a *theoretical* point of view human actors encode things with significance, from a

methodological point of view it is the things-in-motion that illuminate their human and social context.

(1986, p. 5)

Particular meanings are thus configured through the intersecting 'trajectories' of socio-material contexts and performances of sharing. The discussion in this chapter establishes connections between materiality and meaning in sharing practices.

Intimate Affordances

One particular conversation demonstrates the centrality of the materiality of technoculture to sharing practices. As Darryl, a 32-year-old software engineer, talked me through his sharing diary, I noticed that the logged activities show he often receives communication from people during the early mornings, yet he typically does not reply until midmorning. I was interested to know whether this is usual for Darryl and if so, why he might delay his responses:

DARRYL: When my alarm goes off and I'm about to get up, I check my mail or calendar and then the news, then I get up.
INTERVIEWER: If there are messages do you respond immediately?
DARRYL: Most of the time I respond later, it's just an information dump.
INTERVIEWER: Why do you wait until later?
DARRYL: Because I don't like the phone as a medium for responding, I prefer to type on a keyboard so unless it's a text I typically don't respond. Tweets are different. Facebook is usually just to read but Twitter is more of a two-way. I'll tweet while I'm on the train. I don't mind doing that because it's usually pretty short. I won't respond to emails. I very rarely respond to emails on my phone because I find it annoying to have to type it out so I'll wait until I get to work.

As Darryl describes, perceptions of affordances, intimacy and individual preferences, influence media use in performances of sharing. His smartphone is often the first thing he touches in the morning, illustrating its place as an intimate technology. While Darryl engages with his phone immediately on waking, he delays engaging with others through his phone until later in the day.

Darryl has a number of reasons for delaying his responses related to the materiality and specificity of the device on which he accesses email—his smartphone. He prefers a full-sized keyboard when typing emails as he finds the keyboard on his smartphone problematic when constructing extended responses of more than a few words. The repetitive strain of typing using a single digit combined with the compact screen estate, which limits the amount of text that can be displayed, are material barriers. This is at odds to the promise of 'anytime, anywhere' accessibility such devices typically offer. While it is indeed possible to access and respond to emails on smartphones anytime and anywhere, Darryl does not always wish to make use of these affordances.

Darryl's reasons for delaying his responses are not only material. He also indicates an affective reason, based on his feelings about the device: 'I don't like the phone as a medium for responding' (Darryl). He is not comfortable utilising the particular affordances of the device. He is not alone is this feeling. Darryl's resistance to these mediated affordances represents a trend in my research—animosity towards particular technologies that enable (or are necessary for) sharing. As this example shows, participants navigate material affordances and relationships with particular devices and interfaces in order to share. The complexities and idiosyncrasies of navigating these are now explored.

Interfaces

Instantaneity

Interfaces connect 'humans with the intelligent machines that are our collaborators in making, storing, and transmitting informational processes and objects' (Hayles 2005, p. 33). Email (somewhat surprisingly, given the popularity of social media) emerged in my data as a persistent interface for sharing information, processes and objects. I think it important to discuss email as an interface for sharing because of this persistence, and to emphasise that tensions in mediated sharing practices precede and are not unique to social media or 'smart' technologies.

Email interfaces are subtly unique in their affordances (Milne 2010, p. 155). Furthermore, each person perceives the affordances of email specific to her own needs or circumstance, yet common assumptions exist around its convenience, such as temporality and the expectation that, in particular contexts, email demands 'instantaneous attention' (Nansen et al. 2010, p. 139). Yet as an asynchronous medium, an email can be sent regardless of whether the recipient is online, allowing each person to engage in an exchange at his or her own convenience. For instance, Jason, a 35-year-old freelance writer, explains how he used email to coordinate a group activity:

> On Sunday a group of us organised to go for a trail run at Arthur's Seat. Most of these people have desk jobs and the easiest way to catch them is to leave an email to let them reply in their own time.
>
> (Jason)

The group coordinated two carloads of people to meet at a designated place. The group selected email as the preferred means of contact because it enabled sharing with many recipients simultaneously. Email provides the means to designate multiple recipients to a single email, providing an effective and efficient means of sharing information rapidly to varied groups of people. Also, the full exchange was on email rather than split across multiple media channels, which enabled participants to view the entire conversation between members of the group and access what had previously been shared. Although the email can be sent to multiple recipients, Jason has little control over receipt of the email:

> The email text is never realised on the receiver's computer in the same way as it was on the sender's. It is accessed via programs that enable display (meaning, of course, possible confusions of code or formatting in the translation of 'writing' by different programs, but even when there are no such errors, the writing is inherently remediated) . . .
>
> (Klich 2013, p. 119)

Depending on the email program and device on which the email is viewed, each recipient may view the email in a different format. Some may view it as one in a sequence of threaded conversations; others will view emails chronologically, interspersed with other conversations. These functional aspects affect the way in which the email is encountered and responded to.

Because people can reply 'in their own time', Jason considers email to be more convenient and less obtrusive than phone calls. However, it also presents the possibility of waiting longer for a response. In illustration of this, Christopher, a 37-year-old graphic designer, often has to wait for his clients to respond to his emails:

> I get to work and I start my work at the start of the day and my client Rob starts his work at the start of the day, but his work is consulting so he doesn't check his email until 3 o'clock.
>
> (Christopher)

Since clients can respond to his emails when it is most convenient to them, Christopher has to wait much of his workday for their input on work matters. To circumvent this, Christopher incorporates additional media channels when available:

> I rang Sally about work. Once again I'm chasing people at the start of the day about work and they're not answering their calls because they're in meetings or they're doing something else. I get used to doing that. So, as well as calling her mobile, which rang out, I sent her a text saying 'please call', which took me a couple of minutes. I also sent her an email because I was covering all bases. I thought if

she's at her desk she'll get the email and if she's away from the desk hopefully she's got her phone with her.

(Christopher)

Christopher interprets what Joshua Tyler and John Tang (2003) call 'a responsiveness image', where he draws on contextual cues of previous encounters to determine email responsiveness and adapts his practices appropriately. Each channel included in his communication strategy requires a specific enactment of labour. For example, the affordances of voice mail for performances of politeness are distinct to the affordances of email or texting that 'allows communicators more control over planning, composing, editing, and delivering messages' (Duthler 2006). Christopher takes several minutes to compose a suitably polite text message that essentially says 'please call'.

Far from being uniquely convenient and efficient, email is a single process among multichannel strategies that individuals adopt for sharing. Similar to the necessity of comprehensibility for reciprocity, email is efficient only if it is received by the person to whom it is addressed in a timely manner. For example, Maya finds it difficult to meet with her friend Julia because her only way of contacting her is via email, which she rarely responds to: 'unless I get contact from her I can't really organise to see her so I don't see a lot of her' (Maya, 46-year-old public administrator, in interview, 2011). Clare is also frustrated over inconsistencies in accessing email:

I know some people don't check their emails anymore. That's becoming annoying. Text messaging becomes the way of instantly saying 'check your email'.

(Clare)

Acknowledging that her preference towards email might be attributable to age, and those younger than her may have different preferences, Clare admits that she, too, finds it difficult to check her own email accounts regularly and often has to deal with the consequences of this:

I also do that too. Because I have three email accounts, one of them I check about once a month, I get people's frantic phone calls saying 'you haven't responded' so I know that it is an issue if you're not regularly checking email.

(Clare)

Even though she is aware of the potential consequences of not checking her email account regularly, such as missing out on timely information and delayed responses, she continues to be frustrated by others doing the same while making little attempt to adjust her own practices. Such inefficiencies of email are reluctantly accepted and expected by users in their sharing practices and strategies of reciprocity.

There is a tendency to favour one channel over another for sharing. While individuals have a range of platforms and devices available, they perform sharing within 'narrowly defined repertoires' that are connected to the 'rhythms of people's daily lives' (Taneja et al. 2012, p. 951). For instance, Clare prefers email to phone messages: 'The advantage of email over the phone call is if you ring and they're not there. I don't want to leave a phone message, but I can put some useful info in an email knowing they'll get it eventually' (Clare).

Preparing an email allows a form of back-stage rehearsal (Goffman 1959; Klich 2013), with the performance taking place in the moment the email is sent. Clare thinks email is a more considered medium for sharing, enabling her to review and refine her message before sending it. She can cut, paste, edit and delete text until she is satisfied. For Clare, email offers the opportunity to convey detailed, complex information clearly and concisely.

As Mary Chayko (2008) explores in her book *Portable Communities: The Social Dynamics of Online and Mobile Connectedness*, technologies, including email, can prompt anxiety as 'we attempt to master the "rules" and norms of modern technology use' (pp. 126–7). Such anxieties influence preferences for particular communication strategies over others. Darryl expressed multiple technology preferences dependent on the context and content he wishes to share. When I asked how he is most likely to contact a good friend of his who lives overseas he said, 'I wouldn't use email. I'm not a big email user. If it's short and sharp, then I'll use a tool to do it like Twitter or Facebook. If it's something more meaty I'll probably pick up the phone' (Darryl). Darryl's interface selection process appears at first glance to be based on his interpretation of email's specific technological affordances. However, closer investigation reveals that his preferences are due to residual feelings stemming from an incident a number of years ago where there was a miscommunication through email in which Darryl inadvertently soured a friendship. Darryl lost an entire friendship circle because of a poorly worded email, which was intentionally sent to a group email list he himself had constructed. His description of the incident is central to this chapter's argument and is therefore worth quoting at length:

> I've said a few things online in emails when I was younger that really have burnt me. I lost a couple of really good friends with some comments I made about my travels in my first trip to China. It got taken the wrong way and so I lost a group of friends. I found my first trip to China to be very tough. I had a very mixed trip. I went to a wedding, which was great, but I had such a culture shock before I got there. I found it incredibly confronting and I found things about the

wedding a bit strange. I wrote a [group] email after a few too many beers which wasn't the smartest thing to do, and I worded the email particularly poorly when I explained my experience. I was giving everyone an update about where I was and what I'd done. It [intentionally] went out to everyone and the bride responded to everyone and had a crack at me. It was because I . . . I mean it was her wedding, and it was my take on some of the things that I found bizarre. It wasn't what I said, it was how I said it. I didn't back up my statement with 'the wedding was fantastic, the people were lovely, etc'. I remember when I phoned home my dad said to me 'I knew exactly what you meant, you just said it in an appalling way'.

So I'm very reluctant . . . I've a learned a few lessons about it all. Sometimes you need to not send things by email or wait a little while to get your thoughts together because you can't take it back.

(Darryl)

Although he had constructed the group email list himself, he imagined those back in Australia as the crucial audience to the email, temporarily forgetting that the list also contained the bridal party and others with him in China for the wedding. Had Darryl emailed how much he enjoyed the wedding and meeting the couple's friends and families before sharing his feelings about his experience of culture shock, the email may have been received differently, with less subsequent fallout. Effectively what he chose not to share affected the interpretation of his email. Because of this incident, Darryl is very aware of what he shares online and how it may be perceived. Now he considers his use of particular interfaces carefully and self-censors his sharing knowing how this reflects on his presentation of self. Shying away from group email use, he is also circumspect in his use of Facebook, Twitter and his blog. 'I'm much more sensitive about what I share on Facebook, about my opinions and thoughts and stuff whereas Twitter I'm not. Twitter I'm not censored, so to speak' (Darryl). Darryl has also learnt to appreciate the persistence (boyd 2014) of online communication where retraction or deletion is problematic. To account for this, he tries to be more considered and allow himself time to reflect on what he's sharing.

Interventions

In digital culture more broadly, interfaces shape the sharing practices available. As Jose van Dijck (2013a, 2013b) demonstrates, there is a struggle over desired practices between users and platforms such as Facebook and LinkedIn, a struggle that is 'played out at the level of the interface' (2013b, p. 200). The interfaces of social media platforms structure sharing practices through their information architecture, which is the hierarchy of particular elements and pathways on screen. These identify and highlight particular actions afforded in the interface. Interface structures are distinct from but interwoven with social structures, both of which have bearing on sharing practices. For example, Michelle is unconvinced by the purpose of the 'share' button on Facebook, which is placed under content others have posted from external websites. When selected, it posts the same content to the user's own profiles, thereby distributing the content further.

The 'share' button allows users to post something they see on Facebook to their own profile. In sharing the object, they are making a value judgement that it is something worth passing on to their friends. Also, it encourages *any* content to be shared:

> My friend was talking to me about the 'share' button on Facebook. He doesn't like that because he feels that the notion of sharing is a positive notion that you're giving something whereas he feels like it justifies people to be in a bad mood or look like a loser and put that up and share, so that's a good thing! Whereas, actually, it's not a good thing. It should say 'share positive things'.
>
> (Michelle)

Michelle and her friend feel that labelling this feature 'share' implies that anything posted through this function is coded as being meaningful and significant and that it encourages people to post greater amounts of content to their profiles, which may be contradictory or create 'noise' in their presentation of self. Michelle and her friend's conversation expresses many ideas which are central to this book: the ubiquity of the term *sharing*, the way it is used ambiguously in platform interfaces to mean any process of distributing content and the popular assumption that the term's meaning is inherently positive.

The interface is itself a collaborator in impression management (van Dijck 2013b). As Esel explains, '[i]f you like something it is automatically shared with all your friends as if to say 'this person liked this, you should like it as well' so they are definitely directing you in which ways to share stuff'. As discussed in the previous chapter, Esel questions the way in which her use of the 'like' button is shaped by the algorithms of the platform. These coded 'likes', displayed to her friends, imply they too might like a particular brand of clothing. Her main concern is that it shows no degree of how much she likes a brand or item. The consequences of this are that she is presented as having a strong association with the brand or item, signalling taste that is not necessarily representative of her values. Additionally, as discussed in Chapter 1, the use of 'like' buttons and other such counters are primarily tracking devices providing valuable user metrics, in turn fueling the 'like economy' (Gerlitz and Helmond 2013).

Understanding platform conventions for sharing are as important as understanding social conventions. Regrets around sharing may be related to the disclosure of sensitive content, actioned without sufficient consideration of the consequences or through misunderstanding the interface. Indeed, Yang Wang et al. (2011) observe that people's 'regrettable postings' could be averted 'if they were better able to utilise Facebook's granular access controls' (p. 10). Limitations of understanding particular interfaces, coupled with emotional states, contribute to sharing regrets. Yet regrets are not always motivated by a lack of comprehension of appropriate conventions of conduct. For example, in Chapter Four, I discussed a conversation interview participant Vanessa had on Facebook which she later deleted in order to establish a more comfortable semi-gated boundary to herself. She had posted a status update about wanting to go rock climbing and an old friend who she'd had little contact with in recent years responded which extended into a conversation back and forth across their profile pages:

> We kept forgetting that we were just on comment threads and there would be threads that were sixty, seventy comments long. Completely inane stuff, so not stuff I was worried about anyone else reading. . . . It didn't really bother me that it was all public, though I did delete the thread. I'm not really sure why to be honest, just the fact that there was this long thread on my Facebook.
>
> (Vanessa)

Even though the exchange didn't contain particularly sensitive details, its very banality and everydayness meant the exchange felt personal. It was too mundane to share widely but specific enough to feel personal. While the effect of leaving the exchange up on her page would likely be minimal, to retain it risked signalling an inability to understand the conventions of the platform or a form of arrogance by parading the conversation and relationship it implied.

Devices

Connectivity

Sharing practices carry expectations of accessibility. Devices such as the now ubiquitous smartphone afford access through internet and phone coverage networks across diverse locations. Sharing requires accessibility, although accessibility does not predetermine sharing. The necessity of accessibility provokes feelings towards devices that can enable or prevent accessibility. As Graham Meikle and Sherman Young (2012) explain, 'the price we pay for being able to contact anyone, anywhere, anytime, is that anyone else can contact us—anywhere, anytime' (p. 154). Similarly, Rich Ling (2012) points out in relation to the reciprocal expectations of mobile phone use and access, 'it is not completely our own choice as to whether we need a phone. It is not completely our own desire that is at work, but rather that of our social sphere' (p. 162). Because mobiles are habitually carried on the person, there is an assumption that they can be used to share contact with the holder wherever they are located, and that the contact will be desired. This is not always the case. For example, Jason feels restricted by his mobile phone:

> I don't have a phone at home with an answering machine, I've got the mobile. It is necessary because I've technically said to people 'you can reach me on this'. So if I don't ever look at it I'm basically telling people 'you can reach me on this but I'm going to ignore you. You are not important enough for me to check, even though I've said you can find me on this.' I don't think that's very fair.
>
> (Jason)

Contrary to expectations of connectivity and convenience (e.g., Licoppe 2004; Goggin and Hjorth 2009; Ling and Donner 2013), Jason doesn't wish to be contactable all the time, but because he has provided his mobile phone number as a principal contact, he feels obliged to respond.

The obligation to be accessible by mobile phone is sometimes suspended in situations outside the everyday. For example, when Esel was travelling around Europe, she did not have a connected mobile phone:

> When I was travelling in Europe I had the iPhone but it didn't have a sim card in it so it was only when I had wi-fi that I could contact people. No one could contact me. I liked that. You feel so free, no strings attached.
>
> (Esel)

Being without a phone frees Esel from obligations to share with others, yet it also highlights a routine of sharing out of boredom: 'But then it sucks when you're at the train station and you can't call anyone' (Esel). For Esel, being able to contact people using her mobile phone is desirable when she wishes to pass time, such as waiting for public transport. Michael Bull (2007) argues that people use technologies (such as iPods) to fill the voids in their everyday routines:

> I think people find it hard to sit still and just be there. It's like they get uncomfortable in a really short space of time these days and think well 'I'll check my phone rather than just sit here'. It's tough for people to do that.
>
> (Jason)

Another strong motivation for sharing via mobile devices is to present the self as socially connected. 'Phone fidgeting' is an impulse to demonstrate or signal social status by playing with the mobile phone. Phone fidgeting is also an impulse to check that social availability is maintained. Such actions include keeping the device close to hand and checking it regularly (Walsh and White 2006; Walsh, White and Young 2008). Being without a functional mobile phone can produce fears of inaccessibility and fear of missing out ('FOMO') (Przybylski et al. 2013). Mobile phone devices legitimise selfhood, suggesting in the performance of use, that the holder is actively engaged within social networks. For instance, Clare's mobile phone is a critical device for sharing. Having it about her fulfils a need to be connected because through it she can constantly share what she is doing and where she is. Such as, when Clare is on bike rides she likes taking photos using her iPhone camera and posting them to her Instagram profile so that when she gets home she can read the comments others have posted about her photos. Clare does this when out on her bike rides in order to demonstrate to herself and others who may be observing that being alone is a desired and temporary state.

Dependence on a mobile device for connectivity relies on the device working when it is required. Discrepancies between expectations of functionality and actual functionality fuel animosity towards devices. As Lisa expresses: 'I recently got a smartphone. It drives me insane because I have to charge it every night. I want things to just work. My old phone lasted a week because I hardly ever used it' (Lisa). Lisa purchased a smartphone believing it would allow easier connectivity but finds that it requires greater effort to retain its charge, and therefore its functionality, than her old feature phone. Being unfamiliar with the features of a smartphone, Lisa is unaware that she can adapt settings, such as push notifications, to make it more efficient in its energy use. Lisa's old feature phone was more reliable for her. It hardly ever needed charging; therefore, it didn't insinuate itself into her daily routine. It was a quiet participator in her day-to-day life, whereas her new phone demands more attention, which she is reluctant to give.

Devices demand varying degrees of attention. Using features such as push notifications on mobile devices, which notify the owner that a new message has been received, allows for monitoring of social activity within features or applications such as SMS (Short Message Service), Facebook or, at the time of the research, G-Talk. Push notifications provide opportunities for timely responses which situate the self within events *as they happen* rather than as an observer after the fact. Such indicators of connectivity necessitate keeping the device in close proximity, even if notifications are ignored. For instance, Donna uses the vibration of her phone to detect incoming calls and messages. She uses this feature of her phone even when she is sleeping. Donna sleeps in intimate proximity to her phone, with it placed in the drawer beside her bed:

> I usually get messages in the middle of the night but because my phone is usually on silent I don't pay attention to them until the

morning. When my phone is on silent it still vibrates. My phone sits in a drawer in such a way that even if it vibrates it doesn't wake me up.

(Donna)

So that the sound of the phone vibrating doesn't wake her, she places her phone in a drawer. She does this because she desires it (and herself) to be accessible. If she were to turn her phone off while she slept or leave it in another room, she would not feel the potential of connectivity. Messages 'in the middle of the night' are inconvenient to respond to because she is usually sleeping so she circumvents this by placing the phone in her drawer against items that will not transmit the sound of vibration. She uses the conventions of the phone to confirm her potential accessibility by recording that others attempted to contact her:

I don't get called that often so I am like, 'yay someone called!' I get really excited. I felt I'm missing out on stuff if I have my phone off or I'm not on Facebook or something like that.

(Donna)

Donna balances her desired intimacy against the antagonisms of relentless accessibility by placing her phone close, yet hidden away. This also appeases any threat of phone separation anxiety. She acts as though her phone is inaccessible but knows that it is in fact within reach.

Accessibility

The phenomenon of phone separation anxiety, where a mobile phone is switched off, out of power, lost or broken, is the fear of missing out through being inaccessible and unable to access others. Often these fears are unrealised, as Esel discovered when she lost her phone:

ESEL: I used to have an iPhone and I'd go on everything all the time. Like on the train I'd constantly be on like Twitter or something, but then I lost my phone on New Year's Eve and for two months I had no phone. I kind of got used to not using it.

INTERVIEWER: Do you feel that you're missing out?

ESEL: No! That's the problem. I don't feel that I am missing on anything.

Esel thought that a mobile phone was an essential personal item for social connectivity prior to losing her device on New Year's Eve. While the fear of being separated from the mobile device is very real when the device is in one's possession, social isolation following the loss of a device was not realised. Esel was happy to discover that being without a mobile phone was not as tragic as she had anticipated. Although she herself was not distressed, others—especially her friends—experienced anxiety over her lack of mobile access:

> They wanted to be able to contact me. If they wanted to organise something, they'd say 'I'm going to get on this bus and you're going to get on your stop at this time.' Because I didn't have a phone they had to be on that bus.
>
> (Esel)

Although her sharing practices shifted as a consequence of losing her mobile, the social relationships themselves were not detrimentally affected. Esel and her friends found alternate ways of expressing their social connectivity circumnavigating her limited accessibility.

Measures of accessibility depend on access to and ownership of devices. There are various social pressures to contribute costs towards being accessible. Ling (2012) observes that mobile devices (especially those with smart capabilities) are 'an assumed part of our collective lives' (p. 81), yet this is not the case. A scenario Lisa described demonstrates the growing expectation of internet-enabled device ownership:

> I was in Cairns airport flying to Japan and realised I hadn't bought travel insurance. There was a hole in the wall where the computers had been plugged in and connected but there were no computers there. It was just wifi. You had to have a smartphone.
>
> (Lisa)

Being in a public space, needing internet access and with internet service available but no way of accessing it, Lisa felt pressured to obtain a smartphone even though she had no desire to use the features of a smartphone in her day-to-day practices. While Lisa's reluctance was motivated by a desire to remain unshackled to social media, financial limitations are another barrier. Access to mobile phone devices and internet services cost money. For example, although Esel felt pressured by her friends to replace her lost phone, she didn't want to pay for a new one or a SIM card:

> I had an old phone but I couldn't be bothered going out and buying a SIM card and paying for it monthly. But then my friends started getting really angry so I did get a SIM card for my phone. I haven't really been using it that much or doing anything with my phone.
>
> (Esel)

Her friends were frustrated by being unable to access her, though she did not feel restricted herself. As a compromise, she purchased a SIM card for an old feature phone she had used prior to getting an iPhone. With this phone and SIM card, she can make and receive text messages and phone calls but cannot access social media networks or the internet. Esel balances pressure from others to be accessible against her reluctance to finance that access. Because she cannot access social media networks on her old phone, she makes do by using other people's devices when they are available:

> My mum has an iPhone. If we're going somewhere I'll sit in the car and check Facebook on there but I don't feel obliged to do it anymore. When I had my own phone, I'd set it to automatic. If someone sent me a message it would come up as a message whereas obviously I don't set that on my mum's phone because she'd be able to see all my messages. That is why I don't care anymore. I've become really detached from social media.
>
> (Esel)

By her own choice, Esel's presence on social media platforms is dependent on her access to other people's mobile devices. Her own ambivalence within this scenario indicates her exhaustion with social media, her position represents a growing apathy towards technologies which mediate sharing. Sharing through such platforms now requires greater affective and immaterial labour than she is willing to provide. Without her own smartphone, Esel has shifted her attitude about what being always accessible means in relation to her sharing practices. Her desire to use technology is countered by the antagonism of accessing an appropriate device. She no longer feels obligated to participate or reciprocate. As a consequence, she has found that events on social media platforms hold less interest for her now than they did previously. Reflecting on the fluidity of her sharing practices, she says,

> Most of my interactions are in person whereas I don't think most of them were before when I had the iPhone.
>
> (Esel)

Practices are reconfigured in relation to available affordances, values and desires. For example, Esel reconfigured her sharing practices when she no longer had access to a particular technological constellation. Similarly, Donna sought to change her own practices of sharing and the practices of those she is close to because she wished to use only the specific affordances that were available to her. Donna has a plan with a mobile network provider, which allows her a set amount of voice calls, text messaging and data each month on her mobile device. While her voice call and text messaging capacities are restricted, her data access capacity is greater. She rationalises that it is preferable to share by using her data quota than her talk and text quota. To facilitate this, she encourages others to do the same:

> With my plan, I get a certain amount of data that I don't have to pay for, it's already included. So I try to use G-talk because it's cheaper than text-messages. G-talk was already on my phone so I convinced heaps of people to use it. A lot of my friends already have Gmail accounts. To use G-talk you have to have a Gmail account. It's on most people's phones already they just don't use it. I said 'you have to use it because then it will be cheaper to contact me'.
>
> (Donna)

Donna leverages the affordances of her data quota and G-talk to make her sharing practices as cheap as possible. She demonstrates these affordances to others so that they might make use of them also. Underlying Donna's practice is the assumption that reciprocation of sharing is more likely to occur within the same medium or channel. If a friend texts her, she is expected to reply by text. In order for her to use G-talk, she must convince others to do the same. As affordances are utilised, they are integrated and formalised into new sharing practices.

As Donna demonstrates by convincing her friends to use G-talk rather than texting, the labour required to indulge her personal preferences influences others practices. A significant number of participants identify discomfort or loathing of sharing practices, which orient around particular communication modes, such as talking on phones. For example, Esel rarely gets to talk to her friend on the phone:

> My best friend won't answer a phone call. She doesn't like talking to people so you have to message her. If you call her she doesn't pick up. So she's gotten me having to message but I prefer calling because it is more like, personal I guess. And you can say a lot more like in a shorter amount of time.
>
> (Esel)

Esel prefers calling because she perceives it to be more intimate, and also a quicker means of conveying affective meaning. She believes it is precisely this intimacy and immediacy which causes her friend to avoid phone calls. For some, the expectation of immediacy and intimacy in phone calls signifies a great deal of effort. For example, Heather dislikes talking on the phone because of the pressure to keep a conversation going. About calling her own best friend Nick, she says,

> We can't talk to each other on the phone. I'm not good at talking to people on the phone anyway. We just cannot talk to each other on the phone.
>
> (Heather)

Heather finds it difficult to think of sufficient things to say without there being gaps in the conversation, which result in periods of silence. Also, conveying feeling using voice alone requires further labour and contributes additional pressure. Both Esel and Heather, though they have conflicting feelings towards phone calls, base their preferences on what sharing practices they each perceive requires the least amount of labour to convey intimacy.

Networked Publics

Particularities

As well as material devices, people must negotiate the properties of networked publics, both real and imagined, that are enabled through such devices. Networked publics form how each person is known to the other. danah boyd (2014) describes networked publics as 'simultaneously (1) the space constructed through networked technologies and (2) the imagined community that emerges as a result of the intersection of people, technology, and practice' (p. 8). The relationship of self to networked publics is both general and particular. It encompasses 'three dynamics that shape people's experience with networked publics: invisible audiences, collapsed contexts, and the blurring of public and private' (boyd 2008). Networked publics are always already mediated and structured, although as Lauren Berlant's (1997) work demonstrates, the notion of the intimate public precedes social and mobile media.

Frankie, a café and bookshop owner, describes how general and particular notions of networked publics frame her relationships with others on listservs, early emailing lists, which she has participated in since the mid-1990s. Frankie first started going online in Australia in 1994 when she set up and managed a number of electronic mailing lists related to civil rights. Each mailing list addresses a particular public organised around these issues. Frankie developed her role as mediator, ordering content and driving Australian lists. As Frankie describes it, many people going online in the early 1990s were overwhelmed by the 'volume and absolute US domination' of content (Frankie). She saw the drop-off rates in usage as indicative of people being besieged and unable to make sense of the content shared. People were new to the internet and not used to 'using it automatically as a dissemination tool' (Frankie). They required guidance on appropriate sharing practices, which she provided by regularly posting information and prompting discussions. Frankie would post the more interesting content and summaries of discussions she thought were relevant to an Australian audience.

In Frankie's description of electronic mailing list users, a particular public was offered relevant issues and topics; however, this content was also more generally pertinent to an American following. Australian audiences therefore didn't feel part of primary, targeted public and needed guidance in 'becoming' this public. This speaks to the perceived social and cultural construct of publics (Warner 2002). Frankie contributed to the construction of the Australian public through her sharing practices. She listened to the American content, translated the discussions initiated in American lists and distributed them to the Australian electronic mailing list public. In imagining the Australian audience, Frankie imagined their motivations and desire for content and discussion and adapted her sharing accordingly. Frankie also anticipated and adapted for technological literacies of those new to the internet. Content management on listservs requires knowledge of how the software functions and often needs to be introduced to new users. As manager of mailing lists, Frankie also acts as moderator for appropriate conduct. Like conventions of software, conventions of conduct require knowledge or new learning for uninitiated users.

Many of the relationships Frankie developed with people on the listservs in the 90s have endured 20 years. In 2000, during the time she managed the listservs, Frankie attended a conference in the United States where she met face-to-face for the first time with several people she had met online almost a decade before. While at the conference another participant in the listservs, who had a personal grievance with Frankie, took it on himself to contact several of the American attendees and warn them against Frankie. He did so publicly on the listserv on which they were all present:

> There are people I have known online since the 90s. I went to speak at a conference in 2000, and I met there some people that I'd known for several years online. . . . Somebody from Australia, who decided they didn't like me for some reason, warned somebody who was going to that conference about me. I'd established a couple of listservs and this person persisted in making personal attacks, so I moderated him and warned him a few times. He decided that he did not like me so decided to write to this person overseas and warn her against me. . . . The person had already met me in person, they knew me online as well. I had much more credibility in the online space than the person making the warnings.
>
> (Frankie)

Frankie's attempt to manage conduct on the site provoked animosity from another user. This user baited Frankie repeatedly on the mailing list, a practice known as trolling, in an attempt to disrupt the space, and went further by attempting to destabilise Frankie's relationship with other users. Frankie and the antagonist's altercations on the electronic mailing list were framed by their respective credibility within the community.

Frankie felt that her engagement on the electronic mailing list gave her credibility through 'sharing information, having discussions, [and] the fact that [she] did start the Australian list in the first place' whereas 'making personal attacks on people does not help your credibility, which is what the other person was doing' (Frankie). Frankie had already established trust with this intimate public through personal relationships and her sharing practices. While the antagonist's credibility was diminished by their personal attacks, Frankie had built credibility through her labour in setting up and maintaining the listservs and consistently sharing appropriate content with the community over time. An attack on Frankie was an attack on the practices through which the listserv public was constructed, and as a virtual community, they rallied around her.

Spatialities

Degrees of intimacy are also established through shared preferences towards technologies. For example, Shimon prefers not to use his mobile phone on public transport as he thinks it is rude to fellow passengers who must endure listening to his phone call. Darryl is similarly considerate of others when using his phone:

> I usually don't have phone calls with friends at work. I just assume that they're busy. The only reason I phoned Nick was because I thought he wouldn't be busy because he's not working full time. I quite often receive calls, but what's really uncommon is for me to phone someone and have a twenty-minute conversation at work.
>
> (Darryl)

While Darryl is quite happy for his work colleagues to hear his personal phone conversations because it is within the norms of his work environment, he thinks it probable that others do not have the same availability and usually avoids calling his friends during the working day. Darryl imagines the reciprocal labour required from the recipient of his phone call according to his interpretation of the space the other occupies.

Hierarchies of relationships between subjects and affordances also mediate sharing practices. Technological affordances are assumed to be used only when contacting others who are not in physical proximity or when the spatial affordances are inappropriate for sharing to occur. As James describes, '[t]here's no point talking on Facebook when you can walk into the next room and say hi' (James). James's reaction assumes a hierarchy of spatial affordances over technological affordances, that is, when the labour required in order to broach spatial affordances is minimal. Although this is not 'usual', it often occurs: when walking me through his communication log, Jose describes a conversation with his girlfriend via text message. At the time of the conversation he was sitting in the living room, while his girlfriend was in the bedroom of the same house:

INTERVIEWER: You're at home but you're messaging your partner?
JOSE: She was in another room and she was [unwell]. She messaged me to come into her room because she was going to sleep early.

Because she was not feeling well and did not want to get out of bed, Jose's girlfriend messaged him to request a glass of water and say good night. Jose and his girlfriend had particular motivations for acting on spatial and technological affordances and adapted their sharing practices according to these motivations. This exchange complicates the assumption that technologies are used to share with those who are not physically near. Similarly, Esel's little brother also uses mobile devices to contact others in the same house but uses it more humorously than practically:

> I just got an Apple laptop, and my brother has an iPad so he can Facetime me within our house or to my mum. My mum gets really annoyed, she thinks it is an actual call coming through. So we have these face time conversations within our own house, which sounds silly.
>
> (Esel)

Esel's brother recognises the affordances of his devices and plays with these within the limitations of his spatial boundaries. Esel recognises this and is amused by his desire to engage, while her mother, who works from home, is frustrated that she often mistakes a phone call from her son in a nearby room with an important business call. As these examples show, environmental factors, such as spaces and relationship hierarchies, mediate sharing practices. Individuals structure their sharing practices according to their perceptions of these hierarchies.

Consider the following scenario drawn from the sharing diary of one of my participants:

> Clare is meeting a friend for mid-afternoon coffee. Clare arrives first at the coffee shop where they are meeting so she orders a coffee at the counter and takes a seat at one of the tables. While she waits she digs out her iPad and starts to write a hurried email to a work colleague. Her smartphone beeps and she interrupts her email writing to check the message. It is from her friend who she is waiting for, to say that they have just left their office and will be five minutes later than planned. She texts back then resumes writing her email, now taking more time to consider the phrasing and including additional details. Having sent the email, Clare opens the Facebook app on her iPad and 'checks in' to the coffee shop. She then checks the profile page of the friend she is waiting for then browses through the news feed looking at other status updates and posts. She comments on a photo and responds to two different conversations on people's walls, one of whom is a mutual friend of the person she is waiting for. Her friend arrives at the coffee shop, they great each other with a hug and a kiss on each cheek.

If we are to understand sharing practices, we must study them in the contexts in which they occur. In the scenario described above Clare is sitting in a coffee shop but is also on Facebook and engaging in asynchronous interactions by both SMS and email. She uses her iPad and smartphone, moving from one device to the other and from one interface to another. From the critical framework adopted in this book, Clare's context includes her devices. It also includes the reciprocal relationship between Clare and the work colleague, such as whether one is in a superior position to the other, the reciprocity of the relationships between Clare and her contacts on Facebook, as well as the reciprocity of the relationship between her and the friend she awaits. That she is waiting is also of significance to the critical context. Context is particular to setting or occasion and arises from activity. Clare could be meeting her friend to share news, to console or celebrate, or it might be a routine, weekly arrangement. This is negotiated between Clare and her friend. Likewise, the setting is a place chosen and agreed on by Clare and her friend, perhaps because of its proximity to another place, its ambience or the perceived privacy of its tables. Clare may write the email to her work colleague because it is an urgent matter or because she does not like to sit in a public place alone and unoccupied. As I demonstrate, there are many distinct relations within the scenario which may each have bearing on the sharing that occurs.

In order to understand fully the significance of sharing practices, it is necessary to also consider how sharing practices are contextualised. This chapter has set out how sharing is mediated by the affordances of interfaces, devices and networked publics. Sharing practices are mediated by technological and social affordances, yet perceptions of these affordances are subjectively differentiated. Labour is required when negotiating the affordances of particular interfaces for sharing. People draw on contextual cues and previous experiences in negotiating these affordances. Tensions emerge when those cues and social conventions are misinterpreted or unevenly valued. Tensions also emerge between expectations of functionality and accessibility. As a result of affordances of accessibility through mobile devices, people are conflicted and frustrated by their performances of 'always available'. Being accessible requires attention, effort and continuous receptiveness to sharing. Sharing is also contextualised by networked publics, through which sharing practices are framed and preferences for particular technological affordances for intimacy are oriented.

References

Appadurai, A 1986, 'Introduction: Commodities and the politics of value', in A Appadurai (ed), *The social life of things: Commodities in cultural perspective*, Cambridge University Press, Cambridge, MA, pp. 3–63.

Beer, D 2012, 'The comfort of mobile media: Uncovering personal attachments with everyday devices', *Convergence: The International Journal of Research Into New Media Technologies*, vol. 18, no. 4, pp. 361–367.

Berlant, L 1997, *The queen of America goes to Washington city: Essays on sex and citizenship*, Duke University Press, Durham, NC and London.

boyd, d 2007, 'Why youth <3 social network sites: The role of networked publics in teenage social life', in D Buckingham (ed), *Youth identity and digital media*, MIT Press, Cambridge, MA, pp. 119–142.

boyd, d 2008, *Taken out of context: American teen sociality in networked publics*, PhD thesis, University of California Berkeley.

boyd, d 2014, *It's complicated: The social lives of networked teens*, Yale University Press, New Haven, CT.

Bull, M 2007, *Sound moves: iPod culture and urban experience*, Routledge, New York, NY.

Chayko, M 2008, *Portable communities: The social dynamics of online and mobile connectedness*, Suny Press, New York, NY.

Duthler, KW 2006, 'The politeness of requests made via email and voicemail: Support for the hyperpersonal model', *Journal of Computer-Mediated Communication*, vol. 11, no. 2, pp. 500–521.

Gerlitz, C and Helmond, A 2013, 'The like economy: Social buttons and the data-intensive web', *New Media Society*, vol. 15, no. 8, pp. 1348–1365.

Gibson, J 1986, *The ecological approach to visual perception*, Laurence Erlbaum, Hillsdale, MI.

Goffman, E 1959, *The presentation of self in everyday life*, Anchor Books, New York, NY.

Goggin, G and Hjorth, L (eds) 2009, *Mobile technologies: From telecommunications to media*, Routledge, London.

Hayles, NK 2005, *My mother was a computer: Digital subjects and literary texts*, University of Chicago Press, Chicago, IL.

Hogan, B 2009, *Networking in everyday life*, PhD thesis, University of Toronto, Toronto.

Klich, R 2013, 'Send: Act: Perform', *Performance Research*, vol. 18, no. 5, pp. 101–107.

Licoppe, C 2004, '"Connected" presence: The emergence of a new repertoire for managing social relationships in a changing communication technoscape', *Environment and Planning D: Society and Space*, vol. 22, no. 1, pp. 135–156.

Ling, R 2012, *Taken for grantedness: The embedding of mobile communication into society*, MIT Press, Cambridge, MA.

Ling, R and Donner, J 2013, *Mobile phones and mobile communication*, John Wiley & Sons, New York, NY.

McCosker, A 2013, *Intensive media: Aversive affect and visual culture*, Palgrave Macmillan, London.

Meikle, G and Young, S 2012, *Media convergence: Networked digital media in everyday life*, Palgrave Macmillan, Basingstoke.

Miller, D 2008, *The comfort of things*, Polity Press, Cambridge.

Miller, D 2010, *Stuff*, Polity Press, Cambridge.

Milne, E 2010, *Letters, postcards, email: Technologies of presence*, Routledge, London.

Nansen, B, Arnold, M, Gibbs, M and Davis, H 2010, 'Time, space and technology in the working-home: An unsettled nexus', *New Technology, Work and Employment*, vol. 25, no. 2, pp. 136–153.

Norman, D 1988, *The psychology of everyday things*, Basic Books, New York, NY.

Przybylski, AK, Murayama, K, DeHaan, CR and Gladwell, V 2013, 'Motivational, emotional, and behavioral correlates of fear of missing out', *Computers in Human Behavior*, vol. 29, no. 4, pp. 1841–1848.

Taneja, H, Webster, JG, Malthouse, EC and Ksiazek, TB 2012, 'Media consumption across platforms: Identifying user-defined repertoires', *New Media & Society*, vol. 14, no. 6, pp. 951–968.

Tyler, JR and Tang, JC 2003, 'When can I expect an email response? A study of rhythms in email usage', *ECSCW 2003*, Springer, Netherlands, pp. 239–258.

Van Dijck, J 2013a, *The culture of connectivity: A critical history of social media*, Oxford University Press, Oxford and New York, NY.

Van Dijck, J 2013b, '"You have one identity": Performing the self on Facebook and LinkedIn', *New Media and Society*, vol. 35, no. 2, pp. 199–215.

Walsh, SP and White, KM 2006, 'Ring, ring, why did I make that call? Beliefs underlying Australian university students' mobile phone use', *Youth Studies Australia*, vol. 25, no. 3, pp. 49–57.

Walsh, SP, White, KM and Young, RM 2008, 'Over-connected? A qualitative exploration of the relationship between Australian youth and their mobile phones', *Journal of Adolescence*, vol. 31, pp. 77–92.

Wang, Y, Norcie, G, Komanduri, S, Acquisti, A, Leon, PG and Cranor, LF 2011, 'I regretted the minute I pressed share: A qualitative study of regrets on Facebook', *Proceedings of the seventh symposium on usable privacy and security*, ACM.

Warner, M 2002, *Publics and counterpublics*, Zone Books, New York, NY.

Index

Note: Numbers in bold indicate a table. Numbers in italics indicate a figure.

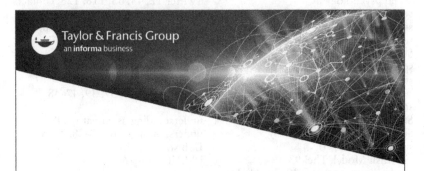

Printed in the United States
by Baker & Taylor Publisher Services